S0-DGI-791

BEHIND THE HEADLINES

BEHIND THE
HEADLINES

at a

𝕭𝖎𝖌 𝕮𝖎𝖙𝖞 𝕻𝖆𝖕𝖊𝖗

Text and photographs by
BETTY LOU ENGLISH

Lothrop, Lee & Shepard Books / New York

For E. B., of course

Library of Congress Cataloging in Publication Data English, Betty Lou. Behind the headlines.   Summary: Provides a behind the scenes look at how a major newspaper is run and put together, the many different kinds of jobs that are involved, and the people who are the various editors, critics, reporters, and others responsible for putting out a daily paper.
  1. Newspapers—Juvenile literature. 2. New York Times—Juvenile literature.
[1. Newspapers. 2. New York Times] I. Title.
PN4776.E5 1985   070   84-23401
ISBN 0-688-03936-7 (reinforced trade ed.)

ACKNOWLEDGMENTS

There are so many who have helped to make this book possible. I am grateful to Professor Howard Ziff of the University of Massachusetts for his generosity in sharing the results of some of his research.

Missy Cusick, then an assistant to Leonard Harris, director of corporate relations at The New York Times Company, was a miracle of efficiency and patience in her efforts for me. Her colleague, Elliot M. Sanger, Jr., and Kate Stone, an intern, were similarly helpful.

John D. Pomfret, executive vice president and general manager, patiently led me through the complexities of the business side of *The Times*. I'm grateful to him and to the many members of his enormous staff who were so helpful.

Arthur Ochs Sulzberger, publisher of *The Times,* graciously gave me, in spite of all the demands on his time, the information that only he could provide. I am so appreciative of the enthusiasm and careful attention to detail that he brought to our discussion.

All the journalists who appear in this book were wonderfully good-humored in allowing me to look over their shoulders, sit in on meetings, or tag after them on assignments. Awareness of the extraordinary pressure of time under which they work increases my admiration for them and my gratitude for their indulgence.

Betty Lou English
June, 1985

CONTENTS

*In many homes, breakfast
is not complete without
the morning paper.*

8

INTRODUCTION

Did it ever really happen—the reporter sprinting into the newsroom, calling over the clacking of the typewriters and the ringing of the telephones, "Stop the presses; this is a scoop!" It is an old-fashioned image we like to believe in because it conveys the excitement we associate with big city newspapering. Today triumphant reporters with press-stopping stories are unlikely to fling themselves into the newsroom. However, I did learn while researching this book at *The New York Times* that sometimes a press run is delayed for a late-breaking story as the reporter files in a race with the clock, and sometimes they actually do stop the presses to replace a plate because copy has been corrected or updated.

Yes, the staccato of the typewriters has been replaced by the more muted sound of the computer terminal keys, but the telephones still ring, the editors still sing out, "Cop-y," summoning the copy boy or girl, and the sense of urgency as deadline approaches still charges the air.

How does that story we read in the morning paper get there? What are the jobs, and who are the people who do them, together producing the material we find in the newspaper? There are over 1,700 daily newspapers in the United States; the number fluctuates as new ones start up and others close down. The 100 largest, according to circulation, represent 74 cities. But while there may be differences in the size and complexity of these papers from city to city, procedures and roles are often quite similar. And although many technical changes have been introduced in the newspaper world in the past few decades, the excitement of gathering the news and writing the story on deadline remains with the reporter. There are approximately 45,000 reporters nationwide. David Dunlap is one of them.

He has been with *The Times* since 1975, but his career in journalism began when he published a paper in Chicago at the age of twelve. "Our circulation was over one hundred, we had a staff of twelve, and when a hamster died, it was a banner headline," he says. He went on to edit his high school paper and was on the staffs of the literary magazine and yearbook at Yale and for two summers worked as an intern at the paper now known as the *Minneapolis Star and Tribune*. After graduating in 1975, he became clerk for a year to the columnist James Reston in the Washington Bureau of *The Times,* then moved to the picture desk in New York and, after a few months, became graphics editor.

While he has had a lot of training and experience in photography and graphics, he really wanted to be a reporter. He attained his wish in 1981 when he joined the metropolitan staff, which reports on New York City, the region around the city, and Albany. "And now," he says, "I'm having the time of my life."

On the fire beat he has developed enormous respect for the fire fighters' rescue instinct, which carries them into situations that threaten their own lives in their efforts to save others. " 'A fire officer's biggest job,' a chief once told me, 'is to hold his men in check. When they see that red devil, they just go.' " He has gotten to know members of some of the special companies, such as rescue and marine. And a large part of his job is in reporting on the administrative side of the department. That is what he was doing on the day I met him.

His assignment is to gather information about the New York City Fire Department's move to its new headquarters. His readers will want to know why the move has been made, how long it took, how much it cost, the size of the new headquarters building, and how the department's employees feel about the move. Mr. Dunlap leaves the office

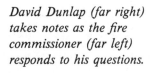

David Dunlap (far right) takes notes as the fire commissioner (far left) responds to his questions.

It takes Mr. Dunlap about ten minutes to prepare his summary on his computer terminal.

Charles Strum and Mr. Dunlap check his story for accuracy and thoroughness before it goes to the metro copy desk (in the far background).

at 10:30 A.M. and at 11:00 begins a series of interviews with the fire commissioner, several of his assistants, and other department employees.

Back from the interviews, with notebook in his pocket and lead "graf" in his head, he arrives at his desk at 2:31 P.M. after a sprint from the delicatessen across the street. A salami on rye and a sixteen-ounce Mountain Dew sustain him as he types out a brief summary of his story in time for an assistant metro editor to look it over; show it to the metro editor, who is in charge of the entire metropolitan staff; and then present it at the three o'clock turnaround meeting. Here the work of the daytime editors, concerned with directing the gathering of the news, is turned over to the night editors (or "night side"), whose job it is to edit the news. Together the metro editor and his day- and night-side aides review the day's stories and decide which will run and how much space will be alloted to each. At 3:20, as the meeting ends, the editor who is handling Mr. Dunlap's story tells him it should be 600 words.

As he writes, Mr. Dunlap confers with his editor and with Harold Gal, the night metro editor, whose desk is about thirty feet across the floor from Mr. Dunlap's. At 4:04 Mr. Dunlap takes a break, and his completed story is called up on Mr. Gal's computer for backfield, or preliminary, editing. Gal explains that he is "fixing the lead, filling any holes, making sure the story satisfies the assignment." Each night twenty to twenty-five stories come to his desk. Now he passes Dunlap's to his assistant, Charles Strum, for further scrutiny, and he and Dunlap confer.

At six o'clock the story arrives at the "slot." In the days before computer terminals, the copy editor's desk was

Slot man Joseph Herrington will assign Mr. Dunlap's story to his rim man, Richard Haitch (far left), for line editing and headline construction.

horseshoe-shaped with the chief of the desk seated inside the curve. From this "slot" position, the copy editor passed the copy to the "rim" editors around the outside of the curve. Today the copy desk is a block of conventional desks, each with a computer, but the terminology endures.

"I look over the story," the metro slot editor, Joseph Herrington, says, "and assign it to one of my editors. He will prepare it to be set in type. That is, he does the styling —checks spelling, punctuation, grammar, and he makes sure that the copy adheres to its space allotment. If he has

Mr. Haitch and Mr. Dunlap confer on the placement of a phrase to make certain his meaning is clear.

*Robert Sheridan's dummy
for page B2 prescribes
the space for text and
photographs for
the Dunlap story.*

questions of a fundamental nature, he goes back to the reporter."

This is what the copy editor on the rim, Richard Haitch, is doing after reading the Dunlap story and converting to brighter type on the video screen—so that those words stand out sharp and clear—any material he has questions about. The two confer on these points until Haitch is sure that he understands the reporter's intention. "A copy editor should be clear that it's the reporter's story," Haitch says. "He should let him have his head of steam. It's not the function of the editor to rewrite the story. That's why I call the reporter over rather than make assumptions."

While Haitch is editing the story, Jeffrey Schmalz, assistant to the metro editor, is making decisions about "play." Originally, the Dunlap story, with two photographs, was slated for the third page in the second, or metro, section, but tonight, because the editors want to stress hard news—that is, reports presenting the facts of an event objectively and in descending order of importance—on that page there will be space for only one picture. Consequently, Mr. Schmalz decides that the fire department story will go on B2. An assistant editor on the news desk, Robert Sheridan, has already prepared the dummy, or design, for that page. Normally, this job would be done by a makeup editor, but because of illness, an assistant news editor is standing in tonight.

One of the art directors, Bill Scott, is doing the layout for the story, arranging the two photographs and the 10 1/2 inches of copy in the space prescribed by Robert Sheridan who earlier worked with the ad dummy. The ad dummy is an 8 1/2″ by 14″ sheet with column markings scaled to *The Times*'s page size and shows which space will be used for news and which for advertisements.

The photographs in the ads have already been checked for dot size in the advertising production processing department. Under extreme magnification, what appears to the naked eye as a solid area is, in fact, a collection of dots. The size of the dot, which must conform to *Times* standards, determines how dark or light an area of illustration will be.

In the meantime, Haitch has completed his editing, and the copy is back on the slot editor's computer screen. "Now we 'h and j' it," Herrington says. This process—by its full name, hyphenating and justifying—is now accomplished by the computer. It produces even left- and right-hand margins almost instantaneously. The copy reappears on the screen in proper column width with even margins. "We're ready to set." And Herrington taps the key that activates the Metro-set machine in the composing room, where each page of the paper is put together. The Metro-set produces columns of print on strips of photographic print paper. These columns are trimmed and placed—pasted up—in the page formats arranged on tables (actually slanted easel-like boards) in the composing room. More about this process in later sections.

While Herrington h and j's the story, Haitch composes the headline to fit the space and type size prescribed by the makeup desk and art director. He tries, "Fire Department Gets Own Building at Last." The length is right, but Haitch isn't satisfied. "I want to get 'Brooklyn' in there." He thinks a bit longer, then leans forward and types, "Fire Department Settles Down in Brooklyn." Herrington approves this one. It's eight o'clock.

Bill Scott, metro art director, shows Mr. Dunlap how he has placed the scaled photographs and the type.

15

THE LEADERSHIP

One of the first newspaper publishers in this country said, "When men differ in opinion, both sides ought equally to have the advantage of being heard by the public." That was Benjamin Franklin, whose *Pennsylvania Gazette,* the historians tell us, upheld this principle. In addition, the paper, compared with others in its area, had the largest circulation, most advertising income, and the liveliest writing. Any publisher today would envy such a record and would be respectful of the fact that Franklin's paper earned a large profit. It is the publisher's money that secures the newspaper initially, and his or her business skills that keep revenues at a level to support the paper's life. As impressive as Franklin's financial success was his ability to influence public opinion. That capacity is one of the publisher's basic concerns and is expressed most directly on the editorial page. But the editorial serves other purposes as well.

The editorial page has been described as the newspaper's personality, and a well-known writer on journalism, Louis M. Lyons, had this to say to a group of editorial writers: "If one needed an excuse for an editorial page, or to try to define the role of the page, I think it would be to express the tone of the paper—this, even more than the policy of the paper. It's a chance to represent the institution itself, as a civilized and civilizing force, as a concerned and a considerate citizen, as a moderate and moderating influence, as a thoughtful person, a good neighbor, one who cares. The tone reflects the character of the paper."

The editorial page as separate from other writing in the paper emerged over 100 years ago, but concurrently, editorial comment continued to be mixed in with news accounts until the beginning of this century, when the idea of objective, noneditorialized news reporting became accepted. Now, ideally, opinions on current issues are confined to the editorial page and to bylined columns and essays.

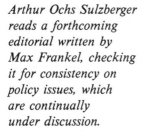

Arthur Ochs Sulzberger reads a forthcoming editorial written by Max Frankel, checking it for consistency on policy issues, which are continually under discussion.

Max Frankel (right) listens to a comment from his deputy, Jack Rosenthal (left), at an editorial board meeting.

At the head of *The Times* sits Arthur Ochs Sulzberger. Under him are the five major departments of the paper: news, editorial, advertising (which includes promotion), circulation, and operations. Because it presents opinion, rather than objective reporting, the editorial department is separate from, and works independently of, the news department. On the day we meet, Mr. Sulzberger sets a sheaf of papers to one side of his desk, swings his chair around to face the computer terminal, and says, "Now, this is where I do a lot of my work." On the computer screen he calls up an editorial that will appear in tomorrow's paper. "One major involvement of mine," he says, "is in the editorial opinion of the paper. The editor of our editorial page, Max Frankel, reports directly to me, because the opinions expressed in a paper's editorials are the responsibility of the publisher, even if the publisher does not actually write them. We have long talks on the important issues. Our longest discussions are on political decisions; for instance, the endorsement of candidates in local and national elections."

Mr. Frankel shares with Mr. Sulzberger the opinions expressed at editorial board meetings. "The board meets three times a week for informal discussion," says Mr. Frankel. "We try to get to the root of the issue. The member who is going to write the editorial gets a sampling from the board, in their questions and comments, of the kind of educating he has to do in his article. When we need more information, we invite people to come in and talk with us—the American Ambassador to El Salvador or the candidates before an election. Each of our twelve members is expert in some specialized area; for instance, economics, law, science, or medicine."

Mr. Frankel became editor of the editorial page after twenty-five years in the news department. "I hang back a long time before reaching an opinion on an issue," he says. "After all, for twenty-five years I was paid not to have an opinion. The issues we write about," Mr. Frankel goes on, "are chosen on the basis of their importance and by the rhythm of the news itself. When the editorial page gets to a particular issue, the reader knows it's time to pay attention, to give an extra few minutes of thought to this. In one kind of editorial we illuminate the issues; in another we advocate action. We aim to set a tone of discourse that stays within *The Times*'s tradition of fairness. We hope we influence people to think and talk about issues in that way.

"Editorial writing is highly disciplined. It demands a shrewd review of the facts on all sides of an argument in only five or six hundred words. Because the editorial expresses the opinion of the paper and not an individual, it is unsigned. It carries the weight of the institution."

In addition to the editorial side, Mr. Sulzberger is involved with the news department, conferring with its chief administrator, the executive editor, A. M. Rosenthal. They discuss policy and personnel matters, and Mr. Sulzberger also frequently attends the news meetings in Mr. Rosenthal's office at which the stories for page one are selected.

There have been many changes in American journalism and in *The Times* since Mr. Sulzberger's grandfather, Adolph S. Ochs, took it over in 1896. But Mr. Sulzberger says that his grandfather's philosophy—"To give the news impartially, without fear or favor, regardless of any party, sect, or interest involved"—still prevails. It is what concerns him, he says, when he talks about his commitment "to setting the tone of the paper and maintaining its quality," referring to both the content of the news and the selection of staff.

While the editorial and news departments are his primary concerns, Mr. Sulzberger's attention is also directed to other areas. "The publisher's office is the place where the editorial and the business sides of the paper come together," he says. "It's here that we discuss the feasibility of introducing new sections in the paper. Suggestions for changes like that can come either from the news or the business side. On the business side, I work with the advertising director and the business manager, making sure that the paper is financially secure—that we have enough money to pay our bills and that funds are being properly allocated."

Mr. Sulzberger is recognized in the newspaper community as being very knowledgeable about the rapidly developing technological changes in newspapers. "Because of the increase in production labor costs after World War

II," he says, "the survival of newspapers came to depend on the introduction of efficient new technologies. In 1974, we completed an agreement with our unions that guaranteed lifetime employment to those people whose work would eventually be eliminated or drastically reduced by new techniques such as automation and computerization. For example, the agreement provided that as linotypists—the people who set 'hot-type' cast from molten lead—retired, they would not be replaced. Photocomposition, or 'cold type,' was introduced. Under the old method, an operator could set thirteen lines of a story in one minute. Under the new methods, stories are set at the rate of a thousand lines a minute. The final conversion at *The Times* from hot to cold type was completed in 1978, but new procedures are constantly being introduced.

"The next step in the new technologies," Mr. Sulzberger says, "will probably be pagination. Pages will be made up on the computer. An editor will be able to move stories and pictures around on the screen. And eventually, in addition to pagination, we'll see the introduction of a lot of other new systems, techniques, and gadgets, making the whole production process faster and more flexible, such as the use of robots in some areas where the work is truly menial. The technology is extending to photography, too. An electronic camera will make it possible for photographs taken in the field to be transmitted over an ordinary phone wire, the way the portable computer our reporters now use transmits copy. The computer has made an enormous difference in the newspaper industry."

But although the computer has changed the technology of news transmission, the basic structure of news gathering and editing remains the same.

COVERING THE NEWS

In the news department at *The Times* there are some 570 people who assign, gather, and edit the news. Under the executive editor, A.M. Rosenthal, are managing editor Seymour Topping and his deputy and assistants, among them the news editor. There are nine news desks, and of these, the metropolitan, national, and foreign are the best-known. Each is headed by an editor who, with a deputy and assistants, supervises a staff of reporters or correspondents and oversees the flow of news to the respective copy desk and from there to the composing room. The other news desks—business and financial, culture, family/style, science, real estate, and sports—operate in much the same way.

This organization applies to newspapers in general, although the size of the staff will vary. On all newspapers, the number of people in the newsroom depends on the time of day. A reporter's hours are determined by his assignment and his deadline but generally extend from the morning through to early evening. Copy editors' hours are staggered: the largest number of desks are occupied as the clock moves closer to deadline.

At *The Times* most desk editors begin their day about 10:00 A.M. and at noon send their list of the day's stories (called the "noon list") to the news desk. In midafternoon they turn summaries of these stories over to their night editors. Supervising the writing and copy editing of the news, the night editors oversee the flow of copy from the newsroom to the composing room. This process continues late into the night.

In this section, I've selected editors and reporters whose functions at *The Times* may have parallels in other big city papers across the country. Regrettably, space limitations made it necessary to leave out several desks and many fine reporters. The subjects featured, however, present—individually as well as collectively—an accurate picture of the workings of a large metropolitan daily.

FOREIGN DESK
CRAIG WHITNEY

Most of the night editors are home at breakfast when Craig Whitney—then foreign news editor, now assistant managing editor—picks up his phone on the foreign desk. He's talking to John Darnton, a Pulitzer Prize-winner who was then *The Times*'s correspondent in Madrid and has since returned to New York City. "Okay," Mr. Whitney says, "if you think there's a story there, go ahead and write it." Mr. Whitney's deputy editor, William Borders, is talking to another of the foreign desk's correspondents—thirty-plus men and women based

Between phone calls, Craig Whitney (right) confers with his deputy, William Borders, who is next in command of the foreign desk.

in more than twenty countries around the world. "Other large metropolitan dailies like *The Washington Post, Philadelphia Inquirer,* and *The Los Angeles Times* also have foreign correspondents, but not as many as we do," Mr. Whitney says. "Smaller papers are more dependent on the wire services, but we use them mostly when we don't have a correspondent; usually it would be spot news.

"We talk with our correspondents sometimes five or ten times a day, depending on where and how fast the news is breaking," Mr. Whitney says. "As for assignments, usually the correspondent tells us what should be covered rather than vice versa. He's there and knows the situation —like a beat reporter on metro. Mr. Rosenthal, Mr. Topping, and I decide about the placement of correspondents, and usually an assignment lasts for about three years."

Along with the editors on other news desks, Mr. Whitney supplies a noon list to news editor Allan Siegal and receives from him the desk's news hole, the space allotted for that day's foreign news. "We usually have about ten stories," Mr. Whitney says. "Bill Borders takes summaries of our candidates for page one to the three forty-five news meeting (in Mr. Rosenthal's office). Then I go to Mr. Rosenthal's five-fifteen meeting at which the page-one stories are selected. Because of the way the time zones work around the world, our copy is coming in by noon and clears the copy desk by six-thirty. Curiously, because of the time difference, something that is happening now in Tokyo, when it's afternoon here, is happening early tomorrow in Tokyo time. So it's possible for us to print tomorrow's news tonight."

Mr. Whitney became foreign editor after many years as

a correspondent in Saigon, Bonn, and Moscow, his facility in French, German, and Russian making him well suited for these posts. He spent some time as a metropolitan reporter before going overseas and feels that experience in departments other than foreign is good preparation for a correspondent. "It's important to know how a paper is put together and how to write a news story," he says. "There needs to be a seasoning process. We wouldn't normally take on someone younger than twenty-seven or twenty-eight. We'd want to get an idea of his or her talents, be sure that she knows the whole operation in journalism. And, of course, that she knows the history of the country she's going to cover and speaks the language. Often *The Times* will prepare a correspondent for an assignment by sending him to the appropriate language and history courses." Mr. Whitney's phone rings. "Oh, yes, don't worry," he answers the caller, "he's a linguist—speaks fluent Spanish, and now he's learning Japanese."

JOHN VINOCUR

Paris Bureau Chief

"When I graduated from college," John Vinocur says, "I went to live in France for two years. I liked it so much, I decided that someday I wanted to come back with a job so I could stay there longer." Five years later he got the job. On foreign assignment for The Associated Press, he was based in Paris and covered stories in Europe, Africa, the Middle East, and Asia.

"The most truthful thing I can say about me and journalism," Mr. Vinocur confesses, "is that I always wanted to write, and I knew that to write well I would have to practice, and the way to get paid for practicing was to be a journalist." He practiced so well on *The Port Chester Daily Item* and *The Long Island Star-Journal* that when he walked into The Associated Press bureau in New York and took a test "to see if I could write," the editors decided he could.

He started as a New York City reporter, then did rewrite, and finally worked on the cables desk before being sent to Paris. Fluency in French and German were important qualifications for the assignment. A number of years later he went to work for *The Times* as Bonn bureau chief and, after five years there, became Paris bureau chief.

"There are three *Times* correspondents in Paris," Mr. Vinocur explains. (Three in London, too. *The Times* has the largest European bureaus among America's metropolitan dailies.) "Paul Lewis usually handles the economic stories. E. J. Dionne [now Rome bureau chief] reports on anything interesting that's going on, often stories relating to life-style or culture. People find France an intriguing place. Its elegance and sense of beauty fascinate people. They want to read about it. I write about politics primarily but cover other areas, too. Over the years *The Times*'s foreign coverage has become more fluid. The editors may move a correspondent temporarily from his or her base to cover a particular event or situation. So sometimes I journey quite far from our office on the Rue Scribe, which is just around the corner from the Opéra.

"For instance," Mr. Vinocur continues, "I was sent to the 1983 Economic Summit in Williamsburg, Virginia, because the editors wanted a European point of view on the

On a brief stop to the New York office from his post in Paris, John Vinocur (right) jokes with Mr. Borders (center) and Robert Zolto, foreign backfield editor.

proceedings. A few months later I spent eight days in Nicaragua reporting on the unrest there. Foreign correspondents are generalists: they can write on a variety of subjects. I enjoy writing about the way people live, the way societies change. I like to do this not from the impersonal, institutional point of view, but to show how change is experienced by the individuals, how they react.

"For some reporters," Mr. Vinocur says, "gathering the news is the best part, but I like writing it, shaping the story. Writing is my deepest satisfaction. When I was at the New York bureau of The Associated Press, a man named Arthur Everett was on rewrite. He would sit there in his white shirt and carefully knotted tie and do a crossword puzzle. Then, when he was put on a story, he'd put down the crossword puzzle and turn out fast, clean, literate copy. That's the kind of artistry I admire.

"And there are other qualities that are important, too," Mr. Vinocur continues. "Being overseas has given me some perspective on American newspaper people. They have a sense of loyalty to the business; not only to their own paper, but also a genuine reverence for journalism. And they have a healthy cynicism about power. They know what's bogus and what's real. They ask themselves questions about things. They're skeptical and curious.

"Curiosity about the people and things around me is fundamental to my work," Mr. Vinocur says. "When I begin at a foreign bureau, my predecessor passes on some information and names to me, but basically I make my own contacts by following my interests. And these come from reading and from becoming involved in the daily life and culture around me. I'm also a reflexive radio news listener, always turning on the radio. And, like all reporters, I'm a great string collector.

"I mean," Mr. Vinocur explains, "I save things: calling cards, phone numbers, interview notes—things that have no immediate use, but I can't throw them away because I think maybe someday I'll need them. Of course, that never works. But once it did.

"When the American hostages who had been held for 444 days in Iran were released and flown from Teheran to a hospital in Wiesbaden, West Germany," Mr. Vinocur says, "there was enormous pressure to get the first story on what their imprisonment had been like. But we just couldn't get to them. Then I remembered that two years earlier I had met one of them in Teheran—Barry Rosen, a press attaché at the embassy. I got a phone number for one of the hospital wards and left my name and number with a message for Rosen to call me. There was one chance in seventy that he had 'saved enough string' to remember me. A day and a half later I got a message at my hotel that he had called while I was out. I couldn't dare hope that he'd try again, so I went out to dinner. When I returned, I found another message that he'd called. So then I sat by the phone in my room. At 11:45 P.M. (5:45 A.M. New York time) the call came. He was wound up as tight as a tick, talking a mile a minute—the first chance he'd had to talk about his imprisonment. I thought I'd have to cut him off so I'd have time to write the story. I finally unplugged him, wrote as fast as I could, and called New York close to deadline, dictating the copy in short takes, three paragraphs at a time. The story made the first edition. It was the meeting of two string collectors."

Foreign correspondents, like John Vinocur, visit the New York office periodically, but not on any prescribed schedule.

NATIONAL DESK
DAVID JONES

"We cover all domestic news outside of the New York area, and to do it," national news editor David Jones says, "we have reporters in fifteen news bureaus out in the country. (That's in addition to the forty journalists in our Washington bureau.) They're covering politics, urban affairs, courts, life-style—anything that comes under the heading of general news. It's important to have reporters on the scene so that they can experience the region, get that special insight that comes from living in the area. It's also helpful for speed: it helps us get to the story fast."

David Jones (right)
reviews a story summary
with his deputy, Paul
Delaney, and assistant,
Jo Thomas, in preparation
for the three forty-five
news meeting.

Each day Mr. Jones is given the news hole that news editor Allan Siegal allots to the national desk. "The amount of space varies, depending on the flow of news events," Mr. Jones says. "We average about fourteen columns a day—that's about fourteen thousand words—and I am responsible for how to use that space, how much to give to each story. Our day assignment editor talks to our reporters in the morning, assigning stories or acknowledging a reporter's self-assignment. Frequently we have suggestions, but it is also the responsibility of the reporters to tell us what should be covered, since they are on the scene.

"In these conversations the length of the story is discussed in general terms. Most run from seven to nine hundred words. If a reporter wants to write more than that, he consults with the desk; there's always more news than we can fit in the paper. Our stories usually are placed

33

in section one of the paper on the pages following the foreign news. We try to cover all major national developments, and we leaven that news with trend stories; with features, which we call 'readers'; and with news analysis. We want to give our readers continuity of coverage, insight into the news, a diversity of coverage, and to keep them informed as events unfold. We don't print a lot of crime, sex, or sensational news; our emphasis is on national issues. When a story assumes extraordinary magnitude, we want to explore it with particular care. For instance, eighteen reporters and four writers collaborated on a four-part forty-thousand-word recapitulation of the return of the Iran hostages."

After sending his noon list to the news desk, Mr. Jones or one of his assistants reviews summaries of those stories with the night editor at the three o'clock turnaround. The day assignment editor goes to Mr. Rosenthal's three forty-five meeting, and like Craig Whitney, Mr. Jones attends the five-fifteen meeting to present his candidates for page one. He receives his copy of the page-one dummy at six-fifteen, and can discuss the decisions then, if he feels an important story has not been included. Between four and six-thirty, completed copy comes in from the reporters. After editing to see that each story satisfies its assignment, Mr. Jones and his assistants send the material on to the national copy desk. All stories should be on the copy desk by six-thirty to be cleared to the composing room by seven-thirty.

"Sometimes, in addition to our reporters' stories, we use articles from 'stringers' and wire copy from The Associated Press or United Press International," Mr. Jones says. "This happens when we don't have a reporter on the scene. Usually it's spot news, particularly a disaster story, or what we call 'one day wonder' stories—nothing to be learned from them in any deeper sense."

Mr. Jones came to *The Times* as a reporter after seven years in that role at *The Wall Street Journal*. Moving from assistant news editor in the Washington bureau to assistant national news editor in New York, he assumed his present post in 1972. "Reporting experience helps you as an editor," Mr. Jones says. "But there are other things, too. You have to be able to motivate people, to be imaginative in conceptualizing the coverage, and aggressive in pursuing the news. You have to have a broad-ranging curiosity. Brains and common sense don't hurt. You have to thrive on pressure. And—oh, yes—you have to be calm in the middle of a crisis."

Irvin Horowitz (left), assistant national editor, presides at the turnaround meeting attended by several other editors from the national desk.

BILL KOVACH

Washington Bureau Chief

$\mathfrak{I}$f you walk one block west and three blocks north of the White House, you arrive at the Washington bureau of *The Times*. It is the largest and most important of the fifteen national *Times* bureaus and "is responsible," Bill Kovach, the bureau chief, explains, "for covering the affairs of the federal government and the city of Washington as it functions as the nation's capital.

"We also provide a Washington report to every news desk in New York," Mr. Kovach continues. "That is, we send each desk the story or stories that are pertinent to

Bill Kovach (right) values frequent informal discussion with his colleagues, which includes a weekly "brown bag" staff lunch.

their area, that are of interest to their readers." Mr. Kovach has just completed the regular morning meeting with his editors. "We reviewed the stories that will be coming up today," he says, "decided which ones we'll pursue, and which reporters will be assigned to them. Out of this discussion I've made up a tentative news schedule and sent it to New York. After they've looked it over, the editors there may call down to suggest some other story. Then, at three forty-five this afternoon, we turn on the microphone and loudspeakers that connect us with New York, and John Finney, our news editor, discusses the major stories, especially those for page one, with the New York editors."

Between four and four-thirty, Mr. Kovach prepares a list of the stories, in descending order of importance, that he considers candidates for page one. There are usually six, never fewer than three, and sometimes ten or twelve. (On average about half the stories on page one carry a Washington dateline.) At five-fifteen, after the New York editors have reviewed the list, the microphone and loudspeakers are turned on again, and executive editor Mr. Rosenthal asks for further discussion of the requests for page one. Then Allan Siegal lays out the page-one dummy, which is distributed to all the New York editors and sent to Mr. Kovach by facsimile transmission.

"It gets here between six-fifteen and six forty-five," Mr. Kovach says, "and since the first edition deadline is at seven-thirty, that gives me time to make another argument for page one, if I think an important story has been omitted. If a story is running late, we call New York to tell them it won't be written until eight-thirty. We handle the preliminary news editing, but the national desk in New York does the copy editing. Nine o'clock is really the absolute cutoff for the first edition, but in an extraordinary emergency, they'll hold for us until nine-thirty."

Beginning his journalism career as a reporter in his home state of Tennessee, first on *The Johnson City Press-Chronicle* and then *The Nashville Tennessean,* Mr. Kovach joined *The Times*'s metropolitan news department in 1968 as a general assignment reporter. Over the next five years he became bureau chief in Albany and then New England, urban affairs reporter in the Washington bureau, and then news editor there. He was named bureau chief in 1979.

BERNARD GWERTZMAN

Chief Diplomatic Correspondent,

Washington Bureau

One of the items on today's news schedule is slugged "Capital," and part of the description reads, "Mideast developments." Bernard Gwertzman, chief diplomatic correspondent, is the assigned reporter. He has been following the Middle East situation for some time and will continue this coverage at a State Department press briefing tomorrow.

Mr. Gwertzman's interest in foreign affairs goes back to his days as a graduate student at Harvard, where he earned a degree in Soviet affairs. He speaks Russian fluently. He began his journalism career as managing editor of his junior high school paper. At sixteen he moved on to school sports correspondent for his hometown newspaper, and later became managing editor of *The Harvard Crimson.* He came to *The Times* in 1968 from *The Washington Star,* worked briefly in the Washington bureau, then spent two years in Moscow, most of that time as bureau chief, and in 1971 returned to the Washington bureau.

Writing recently about his work, he said that he tries to explain "the reasons, possibilities, and motivations for the events around us." To do this well, he believes, the re-

State Department briefings are attended by dozens of correspondents from all over the world, who have an opportunity to question the department's representative following his statement.

Bernard Gwertzman makes a call to a State Department official. The phone is an indispensable tool for establishing and maintaining his contacts.

porter must know the history of the events he is covering. "Reporters need to have a sense of what they are covering now and what has happened in the past—is this event really unique or is it just part of the ebb and flow of world events?" he continued. "Good journalism skills and intuition are important also, but diplomatic journalism needs history as its basic foundation."

Returning to his office after the State Department briefing and an informal interview, Mr. Gwertzman makes some phone calls, opens his mail, and prepares his copy for tomorrow's paper. His background for today's story includes his coverage of the Middle East peace negotiations in 1979, and he remembers that he took pride in writing about the signing of the treaty. Asked if there have been any assignments he didn't enjoy covering, he reflects a moment, then answers, "I can't think of any."

HOWELL RAINES

White House Correspondent

The desk near Mr. Gwertzman's at the Washington bureau belongs to Howell Raines, who is now at the White House interviewing the deputy press secretary. In a few days Mr. Raines will board the press plane accompanying the president on his trip to a speaking engagement in St. Louis. Today, at the interview and at a press briefing, he is gathering background for that assignment. He is also spending an enormous amount of time on the phone, collecting information from diverse sources and arranging interviews.

The area reserved for the press—the press room and the briefing room —is in the West Wing of the White House, to the right of Howell Raines in this photograph.

"Because of the large number of reporters competing for time with relatively few Administration people, trying to make contact is very frustrating on this beat," Mr. Raines explains. "But the phone is an indispensable tool of the trade. Phone interviews give you a broad range of information, while the face-to-face interview is more informal, an in-depth exchange of information."

In the White House press room, Mr. Raines is looking at some photographs with Jeremiah O'Leary of *The Washington Times* and Herbert Denton of *The Washington Post,* when his phone rings. "No," he says, "the briefing produced nothing for the daily." He explains as he hangs up, "That was the news editor of the bureau. He needs to know what to tell New York about the White House today."

Mr. Raines joined *The Times* as Atlanta bureau chief in 1978, after working on five other papers. Assigned to the White House beat in 1981, he soon found himself doing

43

Herbert Denton (left), Jeremiah O'Leary, and Mr. Raines wear the identification tags required for all White House correspondents. Here, in the press room, these and other correspondents have their own individual desks and phones.

what he calls "old-fashioned newspapering." "The day President Reagan was shot," Mr. Raines says, "I was inside the hotel and came out to the scene of the shooting. I started interviewing witnesses, doing my fact-gathering as fast as I could, then phoning the paper, then dashing to the office to write, clearing my desk of everything except my typewriter and phone. In a situation like that you really see the essence of what makes a paper run—people doing their jobs quickly and accurately in a time of upheaval and great emotional stress, knowing that their facts have to hold up."

This kind of excitement might have eluded Mr. Raines had he realized his original goal of becoming an English teacher. But just before entering graduate school, he got a newspaper job and changed direction. However, he did earn a graduate degree in English and holds himself to high literary standards in his writing, striving for the facility with language that he admires in the poetry of William Butler Yeats.

On the White House beat he looks for stories "rich in dramatic possibilities, stories that put a high value on a reporter's powers of observation," because he believes that, "*Times* readers want a fair account, but they also want an account with intellectual focus." He tried to supply this when he was covering the presidential campaign. "Covering a campaign develops discipline; you learn to budget your time, structure your material so that you don't wind up doing everything at deadline. You get to understand the maxim of the newspaper business: the bigger the story, the simpler it is to write."

LINDA GREENHOUSE

Supreme Court Reporter

"Oyez, oyez, oyez! All persons having business before the Honorable, the Supreme Court of the United States, are admonished to draw near and give their attention, for the Court is now sitting. God save the United States and this Honorable Court!" It is ten o'clock in the morning, and the Crier is announcing the Court's entrance. As the justices take their places in their high-backed chairs at the bench, Linda Greenhouse, seated in the press section, rests her legal pad on her lap and prepares to take notes on the arguments the Court is hearing

this morning. First the petitioner addresses the justices; then the respondent takes his turn. A half-hour is allotted to each side, but this morning the arguments are brief, and by ten forty-five, Ms. Greenhouse is at her desk in the press room looking over the Orders—the list of cases the Court has decided to hear, and those it has denied. She will write a minimum of two stories today—one for the national desk; one for the business-finance section.

Dividing a page of her legal pad down the middle, Ms. Greenhouse heads one side "SCOTUS." "That's the abbreviation for Supreme Court of the United States, and it's used as a slug on every newspaper in the country," she explains. The other heading reads "Bus-Gov't." The headings help her divide her notes into two categories, later two stories. "Now the question is whether to offer one story or two to national," she says. "I think I'm going to offer just one. It's the day before elections, and I'm sure they don't have all that much space."

Referring to the list of Orders and to the loose-leaf binders of notes and clippings on cases she senses will become significant, she fills her page with notes. "Now I have to boil each of these columns down to ten words for the sked line"—the brief description of Supreme Court news that will go on the news schedule that Bill Kovach sends to New York each morning. Then she phones news editor John Finney and reports on current cases and those she thinks are most significant.

Carrying a tote bag bulging with note pads and government briefs, Ms. Greenhouse hails a cab for the ride to *The Times* bureau. After a short conference with Mr. Finney, she makes some phone calls, then starts to write

Correspondents check in regularly with John Finney either by phone while out on their beats or while in the bureau office.

her story. She will try to make it not only legal, but also show how the Court deals with issues that are part of the whole governmental process—involving the legislative and executive institutions in Washington, as well as the judicial.

Ms. Greenhouse was first attracted to journalism in junior high school. At the same time, her interest in politics was stimulated by Theodore White's book, *The Making of the President,* which came out when she was in high school. "I was crazy about John Kennedy, and the idea that political reporters could travel with the candidates on their campaigns, could get that close to the important people and issues in the country—that made an enormous impression on me," she says.

It led to her decision to major in American government at Radcliffe and to an editorship on *The Harvard Crimson.* After graduation she became assistant for a year to the executive editor at *The Times,* and then joined the metropolitan staff. She had been *The Times*'s bureau chief in Albany, the capital of New York State, for two years when she accepted a Ford Foundation scholarship for a year's study at Yale Law School. The scholarship was established for journalists reporting on legal affairs.

Instead of returning to Albany at the end of her law study, she joined *The Times*'s Washington bureau. "Going from the hurly-burly of political reporting in Albany to the Supreme Court in Washington was very unnerving at first; it's so quiet here. I went from dealing with people to dealing with paper. But in Albany I couldn't delve into the substance of issues. Here I can. And I like being able to combine that with the skill that journalism demands: being able to organize material on deadline. Some days the Court hands down six, seven, or eight opinions at ten o'clock in the morning. I have to file my story by six-thirty that evening, and I want the material to be accessible to people who have no legal background. I want them to understand the issues. That's the important part of my job."

METROPOLITAN DESK
PETER MILLONES

The metropolitan news department takes up much more space in *The Times* newsroom in New York City than do the national or foreign departments. Editor Peter Millones's staff covers the metropolitan area, which includes New York City, the region around the city, and Albany. Mr. Millones's job is comparable to that of the national and foreign editors, and similarly his desk includes a deputy editor and several assistant editors. One of these is assignment editor Barbara Basler.

"On smaller papers the city editor handles the assignments," Mrs. Basler says, "but our department is so big, it needs someone who does only assignments. I do the city —we have more than ninety reporters—and someone else does the regional and Albany assignments. I have to shuffle a lot of paper—there's so much material coming in that needs to be sifted through to see what should be covered. At 5:30 P.M. the daybook from the wire services comes out. It's a list of the next day's activities. For instance: a bike marathon to benefit a charity; the opening of a street fair; a model boat race on Conservatory Pond in Central Park. I check it, make up my tentative assignment list, and send a copy to the photo desk so that they know where to assign photographers. Then the next morning I call up my list on my computer, have a printout by ten o'clock, and can start assigning. Most of these stories are for general assignment reporters since the beat reporters (police, transportation, City Hall, hospitals, education, and so on) usually come up with their own. General assignment reporters prefer covering a variety of stories rather than concentrating on one area as the beat reporters do. On a big story everyone on the desk consults with Peter on the assignment and on the number of reporters we should send.

"In addition to working from the daybook, I'm responsible for daily breaking stories. For instance, the other day Len Buder called from police headquarters with a preliminary report of eight people dead in a bombing. Should I send a reporter or wait for confirmation? Sometimes you have to gamble. I decided to wait five minutes and then check back with Len. This time it turned out to be a false report.

"Some stories can appropriately be covered by metro or some other desk, like the race up the steps at the Empire

Peter Millones (center) spends a considerable part of his day supervising his large staff of reporters, whose desks stretch in long rows down the metro section of the T-shaped newsroom.

51

State Building. I check with sports; if they don't do it, we do. Sometimes we have one or more reporters on a late-breaking spot news story phoning in their raw copy in short takes to a rewrite person who organizes the material against deadline.

"At noon we send our list of the day's stories—it runs eight to ten stories—to the news desk. We receive the reporters' summaries between two-thirty and three, and I take them to the three o'clock turnaround. Stories that are candidates for page one are presented at the three forty-five news meeting by one of Peter's assistants, and then again at the five-fifteen meeting by Peter.

"From the turnaround until six-thirty, when my day ends, I talk with reporters about upcoming stories, ask them for their ideas, listen to their complaints. Before I came to *The Times* I worked on papers in other cities for ten years. Then I was a reporter here on the metro desk for three and a half years before I became assignment editor. So I know the sources to direct reporters to, especially inexperienced reporters. And I try to match personalities to stories—who would like this one and do a good job with it? I just can't imagine being in this job without having been a reporter."

While Barbara Basler checks her assignment list, the national desk, to her left along the back wall, is just beginning its day's work.

LEONARD BUDER

Police Reporter

𝔍n his office at police headquarters, Leonard Buder is
on the phone with Officer Frank Dunne at the department's Public Information Office. "Frank, what do you
have on that fire or explosion in a Lebanese restaurant in
Brooklyn? Still under the jurisdiction of the Fire Department? Okay. Thanks, Frank." Now he calls Assistant Fire
Commissioner John Mulligan. "What about this restaurant fire, John? Where did it break out? Is this a fire or a
bomb? A fire. You're ruling it arson. Hold on; I want to
read you the wire copy to make sure they've got every-

Even though Mr. Buder can get all of the information he needs through phone interviews, he prefers visiting the site of the event that he is covering.

thing. 'One woman dead; one person overcome by smoke.'" Because the information is incomplete, Mr. Buder calls Emergency Medical Services, a city agency supplying ambulance service. "How many people were taken to the hospital?"

He hangs up, files the information gathered so far, then shrugs into his coat and walks across the street to City Hall to interview the police commissioner at the mayor's press conference. After adding the commissioner's remarks to his notes, he checks his watch and sees that there is still time before deadline to visit the site of the fire. His shoes crunching on the broken glass that glistens on the sidewalk, he surveys the burned-out restaurant and talks to the officer on duty, then returns to headquarters to complete his story.

Mr. Buder, a native New Yorker, came on the police beat in 1977 but has been a *Times* reporter since 1948. "I was always attracted to journalism," he remembers. "When I was seven or eight years old, I would get big sheets of paper from the grocery store, fold them to the size of *The Times,* and hand-print a newspaper." Mr. Buder's first professional appearance, however, was not as a reporter but as a cartoonist in *The Hobo News.* He was fourteen years old. Three and a half years later he had his first byline in *The Times.* Working as a copy boy while going to college at night, he attracted the notice of Jack Gould, who was *The Times*'s radio and TV critic. "He taught me to write," says Mr. Buder, who proved to be such a good student that he went on to win a number of awards, one for his series on scandals in the school construction program. "The story went on for five months, and while it was a very gratifying project, it also became a source of sadness for me; as I dug into it I found that I had to report on improprieties committed by a man who was a good friend of mine."

Today's story was spot news reporting, but much of Mr. Buder's time is spent in gathering police information from his contacts in the Police Department. "I had never been inside police headquarters until the day I started here," he says, "but now I'm in touch with dozens of people, getting confidential information that I might not be able to use for weeks." The trust that police officers extend to Mr. Buder is a reflection of their recognition of his respect for their integrity.

While it's not unusual for his sleep to be interrupted by an early-morning phone tip on a story he's following, Mr. Buder still has energy for his duties as president of the New York Press Club and as adjunct professor of communications at Hunter College in New York. One of the assignments he might give his students is to rewrite "The Pied Piper of Hamelin" as a straight news story. Two of his former pupils are now reporters on *The New York Post,* and perhaps they share his feelings about the job: "It's exhilarating to work on a breaking story. I thrive on the excitement and pressure. And no matter how many by-lines you've had, you still get a thrill out of picking up the paper and seeing your story."

When he has completed his phone call, Leonard Buder will move to a nearby computer terminal, here in his office at police headquarters, to file these notes.

DAVID BIRD

General Assignment Reporter

One woman holds a tiger cat, another a pair of sleepy calico kittens. They have come to the Adopt-A-Pet department at the American Society for the Prevention of Cruelty to Animals, where a program offering pets to elderly people is being inaugurated. David Bird is there to gather information about the project for a weekday column, "New York Day by Day."

"I'm David Bird from *The New York Times*. Are you thinking about adopting this dog?" he asks a woman who is reaching out to pet a lively mixed terrier. He adds her

David Bird's work on the "New York Day by Day" column gives him contacts with a variety of people in wide-ranging settings.

answer to his notes, and after talking with some of the other people who are trying to decide which animals to take into their homes, he slips his notebook into his pocket and heads downtown to his next assignment.

In Dag Hammarskjold Plaza opposite the United Nations, more than one hundred Filipinos have gathered for the unveiling of a ten-foot-high statue of Benigno Aquino, the opposition leader who was assassinated when he returned to the Philippines in 1983. After interviewing the man who heads the Philippine opposition movement in this country, Mr. Bird watches the unveiling ceremony, then walks crosstown to *The Times* office to write his two items.

57

"Susan Anderson and I work together on the column," he explains. "Each day in the late afternoon we go over the advance material on stories we might cover the next day. Some of this comes directly to us, some from the assignment editor." As a general assignment reporter, Mr. Bird regularly fills in on "Day by Day." "I'll be doing it for about three weeks, telling what's happening in New York, what life in the city is like."

A beat reporter is responsible for one area; what is the range of stories a general assignment reporter covers? "It's limitless," Mr. Bird says. "One day I'll be writing about controversial statements from two men prominent in New York politics, and the next I'll be writing on the Three Mile Island trial. But whatever the story," Mr. Bird continues, "I try to get to the underlying issues and to the motives of the people involved. I like general assignment because it offers the opportunity to study an endless variety of situations and to talk to all kinds of people.

"I always wanted to be a newspaper writer," Mr. Bird says, "and I always wanted to be at *The Times.*" He arrived there thirty years ago. Before that, he had edited his college paper at Antioch, published a weekly paper in

Holding a folder of information distributed to the press, Mr. Bird interviews the leader of the Philippine opposition movement. They stand near a photograph of Benigno Aquino.

58

Woodstock, New York, and worked as a reporter and editor in other New York City dailies as well as papers in Chicago, Washington, D.C., and New Jersey. At *The Times* he began as a deskman on the Sunday section, The Week in Review, and after ten years there became assistant science editor. Then, out of his interest in environmental issues, he created the environment beat and a number of years later moved to the health and hospitals beat.

He has now been on general assignment for eight years. One of his stories involved flying through a blizzard from Toronto to Buffalo in a chartered four-seater plane. "We finally got clearance to land," Mr. Bird says, "although the pilot had some difficulty dodging the snowplows on the field. Because communications in the snowbound city were so disrupted, I was afraid I wouldn't be able to file my story. But the people at *The Buffalo Evening News* let me type it in their office and then phone it to New York. When I'd left New York on this assignment, I thought it would be a simple overnight trip. It lasted a week.

"Sometimes when I'm working on an assignment," Mr. Bird says, "I think, 'This is a story that will write itself.' That's a dangerous thought. There are times when it works best for me to outline my copy away from the distractions of the office. I get a sandwich and walk out to a pier on the Hudson to think about how to do the story.

"A journalist has the responsibility to try to get to the truth by pursuing all sides of the story, then writing it clearly so that the reader can make informed decisions on the issues," Mr. Bird says.

NEAL BOENZI

Metro Staff Photographer

"Every shot I've taken could be improved. I'm never satisfied." Neal Boenzi is focusing with his Nikon. His Leica is in his camera bag. "No," he says, "I don't like the perspective. I can get a better shot from across the lake." And he does. His photograph of Belvedere Castle will illustrate metro reporter Deirdre Carmody's story on the restoration of the castle and other structures in Central Park. During a three-hour walk, he visits all of the sites Ms. Carmody has marked on a map of the park.

As he approaches each location, he studies the way the light strikes it, squints against the haze, attaches an orange filter, crouches or climbs onto a rock, searching for the perfect angle. Finally, when his eye is satisfied, the shutter snaps. "Too many photographers have their brains in their fingers—click, click, click. I try to illustrate the story in the best possible way. I want to convey to the reader the mood of what's happening, not just the factual event."

His insistence on the highest professional standards has won him the respect of his colleagues and a long list of prizes, including a record four awards in one year from the New York Press Photographers Association. How did he learn?

"When I got out of the Marines in 1946, I found a job as an office boy at *The Times* for thirty dollars a week," Mr. Boenzi recalls. "I was extremely inquisitive, putting my nose in everyone's business. I became interested in photography and got to be a 'squeegie boy,' the one who wipes the prints to give them a glossy finish. I kept asking questions of the photographers, and after a year and a half, I was on the staff."

Now he's balancing on a gnarled tree root, framing a shot with a wide-angle lens on his Leica. "I like the range finder because of the quiet shutter and because I can shoot at much slower speeds; you don't get the vibration you have in the single-lens reflex." He uses long lenses, 85 millimeter and 180 millimeter on his Nikon. "I never use a 50 millimeter. You don't want to be in a position where you have to shoot from in back of someone." In his bag he has ten rolls of film, a flash attachment, a hand light meter, an extender for his 180 millimeter lens, and a two-way radio that keeps him in constant communication with the office.

Taking the pictures is just the beginning of his job. In

Neal Boenzi experiments with many perspectives of Central Park's Belvedere Castle in order to find the photograph that will best tell the story of its restoration.

61

Mr. Boenzi uses a magnifier to check the content and clarity of his negatives, which were developed in the darkroom just a few feet from the light box.

the photo lab he checks the developed film on the light box and uses a clipper to mark the frames he wants printed. Then the picture editor, Carolyn Lee, will make her choice from these prints. If she thinks the picture is a candidate for page one, it is tacked on the "page one board" that is taken into the three forty-five news conference.

Mr. Boenzi is joined briefly by Dith Pran, who stops in the lab on his way to an assignment. A Cambodian, Dith Pran was brought to this country a few years ago by *Times* columnist Sydney Schanberg, who had earlier been one of the newspaper's correspondents in Southeast Asia. Mr. Schanberg and Mr. Dith had worked together and, in fact, had almost been killed, in the Cambodian war. The story of their friendship and of Dith Pran's escape from the

Mr. Boenzi selects the negatives he wants printed by clipping the edge of those frames.

A photo editor has tacked Mr. Boenzi's photograph on the "page one board."

Khmer Rouge became the subject of an acclaimed film, "The Killing Fields."

Trained as a staff photographer by Mr. Boenzi, Mr. Dith is still subject to his teacher's teasing critiques. "Let's see your negatives," he says. "Are they in focus?" He points to an eye chart on the wall. "See? I hung that there and told him to practice reading it to sharpen his focus. So now, when he doesn't like *my* shots"—he raises an eyebrow at his former student while Mr. Dith grins at him — "he says to me, 'Neal, you'd better read the eye chart.'"

Mr. Boenzi's assignment today presented only mild hazards (sunburn, muddy shoes) compared to others he has faced. He has been all over the world, but one of his most dramatic experiences happened in New York.

He was covering a demonstration on Wall Street when a dissident to the demonstration gave him a rabbit punch on the back of the neck. Becoming so involved in hitting back, he forgot to take pictues. "But the next day I was on page one of *The Mirror*—a picture of me fighting.

"You never know what's going to happen. It's really like that quotation, 'Every day is a fresh beginning; every morn is the world made new.'"

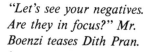

"Let's see your negatives. Are they in focus?" Mr. Boenzi teases Dith Pran.

CULTURAL NEWS
WILLIAM HONAN

William Honan, cultural editor, has just completed a phone conversation with the undersecretary of the Institute of Anthropology and History in Guatemala. He is making arrangements to send his art critic, Grace Glueck, to report on an important archaeological dig in northeastern Guatemala. "Reviews of cultural events—concerts, plays, films, and so on—are a large part of our department's work," Mr. Honan says, "but we also cover this kind of cultural news. Grace will be on the site of the dig," he continues, "sending us reports of the discoveries and the meanings anthropologists attach to them. We have a commitment to show our readers the implications of a cultural event. What is its meaning in the history of human achievement in the arts?

"Our critics are like beat reporters," Mr. Honan explains. "They come up with their own ideas, but sometimes I suggest a project to one of them. That's the fun of being an editor, matching an idea to a writer." There are some sixty-five people in Mr. Honan's department (this number includes editors, critics, reporters, and secretaries). Daily columns, reviews, and news stories ranging from arts to entertainment are written here. "In our reviews," Mr. Honan says, "our overriding concern is with the standard of fairness. Arthur Gelb, deputy managing editor, insists on this. A bad review is told with sadness, never with delight."

William Honan types a memo to one of his reporters. His staff produces approximately sixteen columns daily.

JOHN ROCKWELL

Music Critic

On Fifty-second Street just west of Broadway, the Roseland marquee is a bright patch of light above the nighttime street. John Rockwell gets out of the cab he has taken from a classical concert uptown and pauses to exchange a few words with some young rock fans before going inside. Because there are so many concerts in New York, and because Mr. Rockwell reviews all kinds of music, it is not unusual for him to attend two concerts in one evening. The night the Philadelphia Orchestra performed at Avery Fisher Hall was one of his more leisurely evenings—just one concert to cover.

Mr. Rockwell grew up in San Francisco, and when he decided at fifteen that he wanted to be a music critic, he asked Alfred Frankenstein, the critic on *The San Francisco Chronicle,* how to do it. "He was very generous in taking the time to talk to me," Mr. Rockwell remembers. "He told me to keep learning about music and about writing." Taking this advice to heart, Mr. Rockwell became an avid record collector (he now has "about twenty thousand"), earned his B.A. in history and literature, and later wrote his Ph.D. dissertation on opera in Berlin in the 1920s. He realized his ambition when he became the music critic on *The Oakland Tribune,* where he stayed for six months before moving to *The Los Angeles Times* for two and a half years. In 1972, he came to *The Times,* starting as one of the classical critics and then adding rock.

Mr. Rockwell tries to offer the reader the same critical insights and judgment, no matter what type of musical performance he reviews. And, he says, "I much prefer praising than panning."

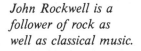

John Rockwell is a follower of rock as well as classical music.

JANET MASLIN

Film Critic

anet Maslin hurries through the crowds in Times
Square to the Loews State Theater to view the first
of two films she will see today. "I usually see one or two
a day," she says. "Sometimes three. I've trained myself to
take notes in the dark. For instance, I jot down lines of
dialogue that I want to quote. My notes are important
because I don't always write my review right after the
screening. If I have three reviews due on three consecutive
days, I like to write them all at once. I usually work them
out at home in the morning, then come into the office in
the afternoon to write them. I can't plot out a review in

the newsroom; the activity there is too distracting. Sometimes I go out for a walk to think through a review."

When she was in college, Ms. Maslin had no idea that she would become a film critic. "I majored in math," she says, "and my first job was at Harvard as secretary to James Watson, who researched the structure of DNA, the genetic key to life. Then I started writing on film for weekly papers in Boston. It was invaluable training. I'd had no journalism courses, no film courses, no creative writing. I learned on the job."

When Ms. Maslin moved to New York, she wrote music reviews for *New Times* and *Rolling Stone.* "I was an avid rock and roll listener," she says. "Then, out of the blue, *Newsweek* called. In 1977, when I'd been doing film reviews there for a year, I got a call from *The Times,* also out of the blue.

"Vincent Canby and I do all of the film coverage. That's a lot for two people in New York City. In my reviews I try to do two things at once: make an absolute judgment on the merits of the film and try to answer the reader's question, 'Should I go to see it?' "

Sometimes Ms. Maslin views films in theaters, sometimes in screening rooms that are rented by film producers in various buildings in town. "There may be twenty-five people or only five people at a screening. For comedies and adventure films, producers like critics to be part of a large theater audience rather than to view the film at a private screening, but I remember laughing out loud at a comedy although I was the only one at the screening. The only thing I don't like about this job is having to sit through to the end of a bad film. But I do love going to the movies. I even go when I'm on vacation."

CHRISTOPHER LEHMANN-HAUPT

Book Critic

There are shelves everywhere, but the books overflow them and gather in stacks on the windowsills, the desk, the floor, on the squished-down cushions of the long leather couch—on any surface that is offered. In fact, they threaten to spill into the small space left for the big man who leans back in his chair, stretches his legs out to rest his heels on the edge of the couch, and opens one more book.

Three days this week and two days next, Christopher Lehmann-Haupt's book reviews will appear in *The Times*.

In preparing his selections for this continuing three-and-two rotation, he will either skim or read two books, on the average, for each one reviewed. Having made his choices, typically he might start a book, a lengthy biography, on Thursday night, and write his column Saturday night; then begin a second book on Sunday, the review to be written Monday; and on to the third work Monday night, writing on Tuesday. This has been his schedule since 1969, when he moved to daily criticism after four years as an editor on the Sunday book review section. As he reads, he takes extensive notes, as many as fourteen pages for Henry Kissinger's *Years of Upheaval,* two to three pages for a novel of average length. The notes help him to review the book on its own merits, not the subject or the author. In writing about so many different kinds of books, he welcomes the challenge of trying to be "as wide a generalist as possible," and notes that Charles Poore, who was a *Times* critic for many years, said the job is like "being educated in public."

He calls himself "a deadline junkie" and often works late into the night against his 1:00 A.M. deadline. The first thing he did after moving from Manhattan to a nearby suburb was to time the pre-1:00 A.M. car trip to *The Times* office on West Forty-third Street. Now that he has a com-

Christopher Lehmann-Haupt became interested in criticism and the mechanics of writing when he switched from acting to playwriting at the Yale School of Drama.

puter terminal, his race against time is confined to the keyboard, since, by pressing the appropriate key, he can send his review to the electronic "in box" at *The Times*. There was a period, after the early-morning dash and before the computer filing, when he phoned his copy into the recording room where it was recorded on a cassette tape to be transcribed later, but then scheduling changes made that impractical. He was also concerned about the hazards of voice transmission after a colleague told him about his white-water rafting story in which he was surprised to read that the sportsmen had been "shooting rabbits." He had dictated "rapids."

Mr. Lehmann-Haupt grew up in a home in which books were highly valued. His father taught at the School of Library Service at Columbia University, was curator of rare books, and holds a Ph.D. in the history of printing. He is avidly interested in books and the art of books. Mr. Lehmann-Haupt's mother is the daughter of a scholar who was knighted for his work in seventeenth-century English literature. As a young child Mr. Lehmann-Haupt was read to a lot. Later, in his teens, he enjoyed reading animal stories, among them, Ernest Thompson Seton's *Lives of the Hunted* and Albert Payson Terhune's *Lad, A Dog* along with the rest of the *Lad* series.

After his acting and playwriting days at Yale, and work as a senior editor in a publishing house, he was offered the book review job at *The Times*. He remembers that he hesitated, at first, to accept. Then his friend, author Victor Navasky, reminded him, "You told me once that if you could be anything in the world, you'd be a critic for *The Times*," and he knew what he would do.

MARIAN BURROS

Restaurant Critic

efore she married, Marian Burros had done little cooking. Eager to improve her skills, she exchanged recipes and encouragement with a friend who was also newly married and also an inexperienced cook. Soon they began to copy out their recipes on three-by-five cards to offer to friends who, impressed with the results, said, "You should write a cookbook." It was the beginning of Mrs. Burros's career as a cookbook author, cooking teacher, and food columnist. After seven years as food editor of *The Washington Post,* she became a food columnist at *The Times,* and two years after that, the restaurant critic.

Pursuing her mission of tasting and telling, Mrs. Burros dines out five or six times a week, visiting new restaurants that she feels may have some merit, and old ones that need to be re-reviewed. Her party includes four to six people, so that a number of menu items can be sampled. Mrs. Burros's judgments about these dishes appear in her weekly restaurant review. She also writes the once a week "De Gustibus" column about food, as well as other pieces. (Recently she has begun to work on general assignment, which includes covering good things to eat.)

Because so much of the food she eats on the job is very rich, when Mrs. Burros prepares meals at home, she sticks to simpler fare. In her cooking and in her writing, she is concerned with nutrition-related issues; for instance, how to eat well while keeping salt and fat consumption down.

What if she ran a restaurant? "I would want the kitchen to be consistent in the quality of the dishes it produces," Mrs. Burros says. "That's the main problem in restaurants —consistency. And in the dining room," she continues, "I'd want the staff to be well trained, professional."

So that restaurateurs will not make special preparations in serving her, Mrs. Burros must protect her anonymity. She does this routinely by making reservations in the name of another member of the party, but on one occasion she used a different technique—a disguise. "I put on a wig," she says, "a really bouffant wig I'd had since the sixties. My husband took one look and said he wouldn't walk down the street with me. In the restaurant this awful thing kept slipping to the back of my head. It took only a few minutes for the restaurateur to recognize me. I was so embarrassed—it cured me of ever trying that again."

SPORTS NEWS

JOSEPH J. VECCHIONE

"We have twenty-six reporters covering eleven teams in the big-four team sports—baseball, football, basketball, and hockey," Joseph Vecchione, sports editor, says. "In addition," Mr. Vecchione continues, "we cover all other sports that are of interest to our readers. These are tennis, golf, horse racing, and the amateur sports, both high school and college and, of course, the Olympics. In covering their beats, these reporters report on the sport as well as the team. That is, they write about rule changes, equipment innovations—that sort of

Joseph Vecchione delegates editing responsibilities to several assistants, including Peter Putrimas, shown on the left.

news. We also have general assignment reporters who are available to write about players, managers, and other interesting sports people. Our two full-time columnists, Dave Anderson and George Vecsey, write 'Sports of The Times.' 'Outdoors' is Nelson Bryant's column."

Starting as a copy boy in 1960, Mr. Vecchione soon became a makeup editor, then deputy picture editor, and, in 1978, editor of the special sports section, SportsMonday. Leaving that post to help start the National Edition of *The Times,* which is edited in New York and printed in satellite plants from coast to coast, he returned to sports as editor in 1980. His desk averages twenty-four columns of copy daily; more for Sunday and SportsMonday. All of it is edited and laid out, along with photographs and other graphics, in the sports department.

One of Mr. Vecchione's most pleasant duties is lunching with sports figures in *The Times*'s dining room on the eleventh floor of the building. He remembers the day his guest was Kareem Abdul-Jabbar, the seven foot, two inch tall basketball champion. Riding up to the dining room in a crowded elevator, Mr. Jabbar burst into laughter when another passenger, looking up and up and up at him, suggested, "Hey, you should be playing basketball."

JANE GROSS

Major League Baseball

he umpire calls the runner out, and Jane Gross hops up from her chair in the press box for a better look at the TV replay. Today she is covering the Yankee-Angels game; her next assignment may be with the Mets. But no matter which New York team Ms. Gross is following, she brings to her work a familiarity with baseball that reaches back to childhood. "My best preparation for this job was being the child of a terrific sports reporter," she says.

Milton Gross was known to *New York Post* readers for

After placing her portable computer on the desk, Jane Gross watches the TV replay in the press box.

over twenty years, and among his daughter's memories of him are vivid images of following him on his job at spring training. Each year the whole family—father, mother, Jane, and her brother—headed out of wintry New York to settle in Florida for February and March. The fun wasn't only in being part of the training camp; there was excitement in the annual reunion with children of the other sportswriters. It's possible that Ms. Gross's interest in writing is rooted in these experiences. It's certain that her desire to become a journalist grew spontaneously out of her closeness to her father's work. Going directly from college to *Sports Illustrated,* and then to the Long Island paper, *Newsday,* she joined *The Times* in 1979.

Today she gets to Yankee Stadium at 11:00 A.M. to watch the pregame warm-up and talk to players on the

"Dave Anderson and I help each other out."

The notes Ms. Gross takes during the pregame warm-up may be incorporated later in her coverage of the game.

field and in the clubhouses before going to the press box at game time. Joined by Dave Anderson, who is writing his column, she asks him to look at some copy she has typed into her portable computer. This game is a long one, ending at 5:11 and leaving little time for reporters to interview players, then write to a 6:30 deadline. "You learn how to think parts of your story through as the game is going on, to save time at the end," Ms. Gross explains. "But there are days when that system doesn't work, and you pick up the paper the next morning and realize that the lead doesn't say all that it should have."

Her story completed and filed, she remains in the press room at the stadium in case her editor should call with questions. At 7:05 she picks up the phone and anticipates his comment: "You saw that I had too many vowels in 'disheartening.'" All straight with the desk, she packs up her computer, her case full of notebooks on the season, and leaves for home. For the fans, it's been a day at the ball park. For Ms. Gross, a day's work in the tradition of a great sportswriter.

Two and one-half hours after the fans have left, Ms. Gross leaves the stadium for home.

JAMES F. CLARITY

Professional Hockey

He dodges around the few spectators still standing in the aisle, takes four quick steps down the red ladder into the press box, drops his notebook next to the TV monitor on the desk, and looks down at the players standing at attention for the National Anthem. The New York Rangers are hosts to the Washington Capitals at Madison Square Garden, and James Clarity is covering the game. The men glide into position for the face-off. The referee drops the puck and the game begins.

Using his own shorthand of swiftly drawn diagrams and

Sportswriters develop their own shorthand for recording the progress of a game.

brief descriptive phrases, Mr. Clarity needs only a few pages to tell the story of the first period. The end of the period is the beginning of his race against his first deadline of the evening. A minute before the horn sounds, he is out of his chair and up the ladder, looking back at the ice in case a goal is scored. If you could watch him dashing from the press box, up the steps, through the gate, down the corridor, and into the press room, you might think that this man who covers "the fastest game on two feet" is the fastest reporter on two feet.

He has to be fast, because he has only twenty minutes to write his 300-word account of the first period for the first edition. At the end of the second period he repeats this race and adds another 300 words. The end of the last period finds him loping down the steps to the Ranger dressing room for interviews with the Rangers' coach and team captain. At 10:27 he is back in the press room on an 11:00 deadline for the first run of the late edition. "Now I send the top of the story with the final score, a running account of the game, and quotes from the coach and captain." That done, he leans back in his chair. But not for long. Between now and midnight he'll rewrite the story for the final edition, adding detail that will characterize this game.

"I begin the night at 7:00 P.M. and finish at midnight, writing three stories about the same event. I start with a simple tune, turn it into a round, and by the end of the night, I'm supposed to have a symphony. I like to prove to myself that three or four nights a week I can watch a game and within half an hour of the finish, can write an intelligible account of it. It's harder than covering a war. For a war, deadlines can wait. And no one's already seen it, complete with replays and statistics, on television."

Mr. Clarity did a lot of war reporting as a foreign correspondent for most of his fifteen years on *The Times*. He came to *The Times* from *The New York Herald-Tribune*. Before that, he had been a reporter on *The New York Journal-American*, having started there as a copy

In the Ranger dressing room after the game, Mr. Clarity gets team captain Barry Beck's statement about his team's performance, "I know we're a better team than they are."

boy. He hadn't planned on a career in journalism when he was studying for his master's degree in Russian literature, but his fluency in Russian was a great help when he was reporting from Moscow.

He says that the language of sports is numbers—scores, records, team standings. "And you have to get them right, because everyone who cares is watching the games." He has been following the Rangers since he was a little boy. For the past year he has been following them literally, on the road as well as at home. He admires them for their extraordinary skill and because they are "decent young men. They tease me because I don't dress the way they do, in fur coats and boots. They tell me my hair and my pants are too short. 'Is there a flood in your neighborhood?' they ask me.

"They know that I'm lost without my portable computer, so once they hid it. I was in a panic until I looked around the bus and saw them all sitting there, arms folded across their chests, that who-me? expression on their faces. Reporting their games is like building a model of the Empire State building with toothpicks in an hour, then knocking it down and starting all over again the next day. It's the kind of challenge that makes my mind jump fast."

AL HARVIN

High School Sports

While the runners' feet pound the wooden floor, and the shouts of the spectators echo from the vaulted ceiling of the cavernous 102nd Engineers Armory, Al Harvin stands at the press desk and types his story. More than 200 public and parochial schools in five states have sent more than 3,000 competitors to the 33rd Annual Cardinal Hayes Games.

As one coach leans over the barrier to urge on his runner in the two-mile relay—"Get tough, Pat, come on" —Mr. Harvin turns to the coach from Mepham High

*Al Harvin adds notes
from an interview to his
copy before phoning it
in to* The Times.

School in Bellmore, Long Island, to ask about the racer on his team who has just won the women's mile. He writes rapidly in his notebook, then returns to his typewriter to add this information. Using the telephone at the first-aid station on the sidelines, he reaches the sports desk to find out how long his story should be. Half an hour later, having gathered the results of all the events completed by that time, he calls the recording room to file the agate— all the information about the outcome of each event. It's called the agate after the type size in which it's set. Agate is very small, 5 1/2 points. A point is 1/72 of an inch. All type is measured in points. (The type in which this line is set is 12 points.)

Back to the typewriter, Mr. Harvin completes the account of the women's events and phones that in. Gathering the results of the men's events from the officials, he adds these to his story. His face relaxing in a broad, self-mocking smile, he returns from his fourth trip to the phone, puts his hands in his pockets instead of on the typewriter keys, and wonders aloud, "I can't believe it; I'm ahead." It's four-thirty and he's half an hour ahead of his five o'clock deadline for the first edition.

Now he will record the results of the remaining events and talk with some coaches. He listens to the man from Bethpage, Long Island, complain as he watches one of his milers finishing: "There he goes, sprinting in. Anyone who runs that fast at the finish line didn't run fast enough earlier in the race." At eight o'clock Mr. Harvin will file his final, or "sub," story, which replaces the space-holding material he has been phoning in through the progress of the meet.

"In a track meet," he explains, "you look for records and impressive performance, like the girl today who ran the fastest mile ever by a New York State schoolgirl." Mr. Harvin has been paying attention to records since he was the assistant sports editor on his high school paper. He still likes writing about high school athletes. "Nobody hears about them because they don't get any ink."

But writing, he feels, is less than half of the job: "You have to know how to get information, not be afraid to ask dumb questions. I like to talk to people." Besides coaches and athletes, he likes to talk to young people who are interested in sports, and recently he spoke about his experiences as a sportswriter at the commencement exercises at his high school alma mater.

"Most black sportswriters on the major metropolitan dailies," he notes, "came out of the civil rights movement of the sixties, when papers were hiring more black reporters generally. Blacks were also entering professional sports in larger numbers at that time. Jackie Robinson broke the color bar in big league baseball in the forties. Before that, there was Joe Louis. Most professional black athletes were in boxing. Louis became champ in 1937, the year I was born, and remained champ until I was twelve. He *was* black sports. Jimmy Cannon, a great sportswriter, said, 'He was a credit to his race—the human race.' "

His notebook, typewriter, and the phone are Mr. Harvin's essential tools for nearly every assignment.

BUSINESS AND FINANCE NEWS

JOHN M. LEE

"It's like a three-legged stool," John M. Lee, business and finance editor, says in describing his department. "We report on business, finance, and economics," Mr. Lee continues. "Business includes, among other areas: industry—automobile, energy and others; commerce—retailing, for instance; and technology—automation would be an example.

"Finance, the second leg of the stool, includes Wall Street, banking, thrift institutions, interest rates, and corporate finance, as well as other areas.

"And the third leg, economics, ranges over production, business cycles, employee concerns, and national economic policy as it is set in Washington—tax laws, securities regulations, transportation, and communications regulations.

"At any given time we have between thirty-five and forty reporters covering these beats," Mr. Lee says. "Our total staff of some eighty-five men and women includes (in addition to reporters) editors, copy editors, makeup and graphics editors, all of them working to produce the daily section, Business Day, as well as a Sunday business section."

The general goals of his department, Mr. Lee says, are to break spot news—such as technological advances or Wall Street mergers—and to identify trends such as deflation or the current rash of corporate mergers. "Our concern is to explain, not just report the news," Mr. Lee says. "We want to make it accessible to all readers who are interested, not just the specialists."

John M. Lee stands at the bulletin board where graphic material illustrating business conditions is posted for handy reference.

AGIS SALPUKAS

Business and Finance Reporter

The reporter was standing in a hallway when a confrontation erupted between two men on opposing sides in the dispute he was covering. One of the men pulled a gun. Everyone looked around anxiously—where to run? The reporter dashed outside and took cover behind a car as the assailant came running out looking for his intended victim, who had fled. He saw the reporter, thought he was his man, pointed the gun at him, then caught sight of the man he was after. He shot and wounded him. The reporter ended up writing a page-one firsthand account. The experience of a reporter on the police beat? No. That was Agis Salpukas covering an auto industry story in Detroit for the national desk before he moved to cover news of business and finance.

Mr. Salpukas joined *The Times* in 1963 after graduating from Long Island University and while pursuing his Ph.D. in modern European history at Columbia University. "I started as a news clerk [a kind of paid apprenticeship] on the metro desk," Mr. Salpukas says, "and hit a big exclusive: the plan to finish St. John the Divine, the cathedral on One Hundred Twelfth Street in New York City. My story won the Publisher's Award [special recognition from the publisher], and I was put on the city staff.

"I came up through the city side," Mr. Salpukas continues, "and then covered Nassau and Suffolk counties on Long Island. From there I went to the national desk." After six years in Detroit, the last three as bureau chief, Mr. Salpukas was sent to Washington, D.C., to join other reporters covering the resignation of Vice-President Spiro Agnew and the Watergate story.

"In 1976, I was brought into the business and finance

Agis Salpukas sets up an interview with an airline executive for a story he is writing on benefits proposed for airline employees. Business and finance editors' desks are seen in the background.

department because I'd had a lot of experience in the auto industry," Mr. Salpukas says. "The editors were rebuilding the department, getting ready to start a special section for us, Business Day. Before that, business news had been considered a stepchild by some editors and papers, not in the mainstream. But believe you me, the publisher of *The Times* made sure this was changed here. Now there is more emphasis on writing style: stories are brought closer to the average reader rather than being directed to the specialist. But our editor, John Lee, still wants the nuts and bolts—earnings, losses—the hard facts. Other large dailies are doing the same thing."

Mr. Salpukas has covered steel, chemicals, pharmaceuticals, and now is on the transportation beat. "Because this beat is so widely scattered," Mr. Salpukas says, "I have to do a lot of work on the phone for speed, but I prefer to work in the field. It's more interesting to see people in their surroundings. You sacrifice immediacy and richness in a phone interview. Now I'm working on an airlines story and will interview people at La Guardia airport."

When Mr. Salpukas was in high school and working on the school paper, he met Walter Cronkite. "I remember he said that he never regretted going into this field," Mr. Salpukas says. "That really impressed me and turned me toward journalism. I admire Cronkite because as the medium was changing, becoming more entertainment-oriented, he stuck to the old values. We're still trying to perpetuate those values by organizing news in terms of importance, not sensation, and by writing what the reader should know about."

SCIENCE NEWS
RICHARD FLASTE

Richard Flaste, director of science news, lists some of the areas his department covers. "Medicine, biology, psychology, technology, space, anthropology, archaeology, environment, animal behavior; there's no science we don't cover, and we also write about science policy.

"We have ten reporters," Mr. Flaste continues, "nine in New York and one in Washington, D.C. Each has a specialty, a beat, but is also knowledgeable in other science areas. My deputy, assistant editor, and I review many of the one hundred twenty periodicals that come into the office and sometimes make assignments based on our reading. But more often a reporter will confer with us about developments in the fields he covers, and we decide which of them will yield the best stories. In addition, there is a constant flow of press releases and other announcements that we appraise."

The daily science hole, except for Tuesday, is usually two columns but can be as many as eight. "For instance," Mr. Flaste explains, "when there's a space shot, in addition to a description of the progress of the mission, we might include stories on the astronauts or perhaps some discussion of the mission as it relates to the Russian space program. In Tuesday's Science Times section we have twenty and a half columns.

"All of our reporting," Mr. Flaste continues, "presents science as a news story that touches people and their lives directly—an intimate news event. We take a current development and wrap it into the general picture so that people are educated in the larger framework which at its heart is the workings of the world."

Richard Flaste checks the copy of one of his reporters for the weekly Science Times section.

JOHN NOBLE WILFORD

Science Reporter

When John Noble Wilford was awarded the Pulitzer Prize in journalism, recognizing his ability to convey "both the wonder and the reality of science," there were, of course, many congratulatory telegrams. One of them came from Robert Crippen, the pilot on the first space shuttle flight and the commander on a subsequent flight. Mr. Wilford met Commander Crippen while covering that first mission and has had contact with him, as well as other astronauts, in reporting all of the major space flights since 1965, when he joined *The Times* specifically to cover the Apollo moon landing.

95

Mr. Wilford, who grew up in Kentucky and Tennessee, always knew he wanted to be a journalist. "When I was five or six years old," Mr. Wilford says, "I became fascinated by newspapers. This was just before World War II, and I would listen to the news reports on the radio, then see them in the paper the next day. I realized there was something going on in the world far beyond Kentucky. Soon I started writing my own paper, and for six or seven years I put out pencil-written editions on typing paper—news of my family and news borrowed from the local paper."

While in high school and college in Tennessee, Mr. Wilford worked on local papers. After earning a graduate degree in political science at Syracuse University, he joined *The Wall Street Journal,* where he reported on medical research and the drug industry. Later, after a year's study at Columbia University, he became a contributing editor at *Time* magazine, then wrote the science section and, he says, "I got really interested in science. It was the time of acceleration of this country's space program, and I began to see how important science is in our culture and in the whole world.

"I'm a journalist first and a specialist second," Mr. Wilford continues. "For each story I train myself in the subject; I read a lot to learn the language scientists are speaking. It's hard work writing on science—finding the evocative way to explain something that's esoteric. Hard work, but there's no reward that's greater."

Covering a space flight, Mr. Wilford begins his work with briefings at the Johnson Space Center in Houston a couple of months before the launching. But because he has

As a science reporter, John Noble Wilford is able to indulge his interest in anthropology.

reported so many flights, it is not necessary for him to be there; he can get whatever information he needs by patching into the briefing on the phone. Then, two weeks before the mission, the National Aeronautics and Space Administration puts out a thirty- or forty-page press kit. This gives the time line from prelaunch through to the landing and also provides biographies of the crew.

"Over several weeks before the launch," Mr. Wilford says, "I spend an hour or two a day preparing my background information. Then, three or four days before the mission, I go to Cape Canaveral. Two days before the launch there are a number of briefings. These include information about the time line, priorities, contingency planning, explanations from scientists whose experiments will be carried out on board, a weather briefing, and, if things went wrong on the last mission, a report about those problems and how they hope to prevent their reoccurrence. The bits and pieces begin to fall together, and I'm ready to write my launching story.

"In the early morning of the day after the launching, I fly to follow the rest of the flight at Mission Control," Mr. Wilford continues. "On closed circuit TV in the press room I can watch the people in the control room and can see any TV transmitted from the shuttle. I also get the air-to-ground exchange between the shuttle and control. At the change of shifts in the control room, the controllers come to the press room to answer questions. After filing for the first edition, I go to dinner, then call the news center at Mission Control to see if anything has happened, or I call the news desk at *The Times* to check whether there's anything new on the wire services. I depend on the people in New York who are watching the wires to alert me to any changes. As the time line draws closer to landing, I fly to Edwards Air Force Base in California and stay for two or three days after the landing for the follow-up. By this time I've been working fourteen days straight and filing a story each day, but I build up momentum in the excitement of the assignment."

In 1983, on the twenty-fifth anniversary of NASA, Mr. Wilford wrote an article on the history and the future of the space program. He pointed out that we are entering a period of less exploration and more exploitation. "Space is a place, not a science," Mr. Wilford says. "It's a place to go to do science. It offers the opportunity for studies in physiology, geology, and physics."

Mr. Wilford's particular areas of interest are paleontology, archaeology, geology, and anthropology. When preparation of the Margaret Mead Hall of Pacific Peoples was announced by the American Museum of Natural History in New York City, Mr. Wilford went to talk to Professor Philip Gifford about the design of the hall and the content of its exhibits. "I am responsible for covering all shuttle shots," Mr. Wilford says, "but non-space stories are assigned by the director of science news, Richard Flaste, on the basis of 'when you can do them.'"

One day a week the science department has its own section, Science Times, which is edited in the department itself. The rest of the week science stories are pre-edited in the department, then sent to the national desk for line-by-line editing. Other major metropolitan dailies have science reporters, but a large science department is not common. *The Times* also has specialists—for example, a physician who covers medicine and health news.

Among all of his assignments Mr. Wilford's favorite is his coverage of the little unmanned spacecraft, *Pioneer 10*. "It flew by Jupiter ten years ago," Mr. Wilford says, "and now is leaving the solar system. In the summer of '83 it crossed the orbit of Neptune and is now out beyond the planets, still transmitting. It might continue for five years and show us where the edge of the solar system is. I tried to imagine myself on that craft.

"Reporting on science in space," Mr. Wilford continues, "keeps you young and alive because you're forced to expand your mind and your enthusiasms. It feeds your sense of wonder."

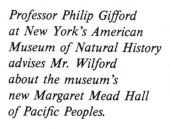

Professor Philip Gifford at New York's American Museum of Natural History advises Mr. Wilford about the museum's new Margaret Mead Hall of Pacific Peoples.

THE TOP OF THE NEWS

At three forty-five a group of editors gathers around the conference table in the office of executive editor A. M. Rosenthal. All day stories have been flowing into the news desks. Now, at this news meeting, the process of selection of major stories for page one of tomorrow's paper has begun as assistant editors present summaries of stories their desks consider candidates for the front page. Of course, not all desks have such stories every day, but representatives of the major desks always attend, with the exception of the style, sports, and culture desks, which

A. M. Rosenthal reviews the top of the news (the most important stories of the day, candidates for page one) at the three forty-five meeting with the editors who present summaries of these stories.
Mr. Sulzberger (left rear) also attends this meeting.

send someone only when a story of theirs is a page-one possibility. News editor Allan Siegal is also present, and the voice of the Washington bureau news editor, John Finney, comes from the loudspeaker connecting New York with Washington. Along with managing editor Seymour Topping (who chairs this meeting) and Mr. Sulzberger, Mr. Rosenthal questions the editors about the news and sometimes suggests further lines of inquiry in pursuing stories. To this process he bring his years of experience as a reporter, Pulitzer Prize-winning foreign correspondent, metropolitan editor, and managing editor.

At five-fifteen Mr. Rosenthal meets again with Mr. Topping, Mr. Siegal, and the desk editors who have stories they think should be considered for the front page. The photo editor comes with a bulletin board on which he has tacked photographs illustrating the major stories. After a full discussion, Mr. Rosenthal, Mr. Topping, and Mr. Siegal meet separately, and the stories for page one arc selected.

Most of Mr. Rosenthal's time and attention are invested in overseeing the news department (Sunday as well as daily, and including the Sunday magazine). This involves journalistic judgments and decisions in which he exercises his definition of news and his commitment to the principle of freedom of the press.

In presenting his view of the journalist's obligation to serve the public's right to know, Mr. Rosenthal has said, "Every day in the year, scores of times a day, editors like myself tell our reporters to go out and get the meaning of the story, the facts behind the facts, to go beyond handouts, to investigate, to cut through the muck of verbiage and find out what really happened.

"We send people out at great personal risk to themselves . . ." Mr. Rosenthal continued in this speech. "We and they accept the risk because we feel we are doing something not only worthwhile, but essential to the functioning of an American democracy, and that is to provide the people of the country with as much meaningful information as possible on which to base their judgments. I have lived in authoritarian societies, and it strikes me that this is the essence of democracy and one of the basic differences between a democratic process and an authoritarian process."

"I am deputy to Mr. Rosenthal across the board," Mr. Topping says when asked about his duties as managing editor. "It's my responsibility," he continues, "to coordinate the work of the news desk—to see that the reports are of a high quality, that the staff is deployed properly, and that production of the paper is on time and in good order. My specific area is the hard news: the foreign, national, metropolitan, and financial-business reports. I also receive reports from the photo editor. The culture, sports, and science news desks report to the deputy managing editor, Arthur Gelb. And the assistant managing editor is in charge of art operations—page layouts and graphics."

Mr. Topping began his journalism career as a foreign correspondent in China and Southeast Asia. Other foreign assignments led to the post of foreign news editor, then assistant managing editor, and now managing editor.

When there is an event of major importance, Mr. Topping coordinates the work of the desks involved. For in-

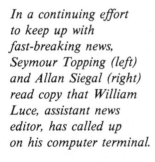

In a continuing effort to keep up with fast-breaking news, Seymour Topping (left) and Allan Siegal (right) read copy that William Luce, assistant news editor, has called up on his computer terminal.

stance, at eight o'clock on a recent evening, the news editor, the national, foreign, business-financial editors, and the Washington bureau chief (joining the group by loudspeaker), met with Mr. Topping to listen to a presidential news conference. "We discussed the organization of the stories on the conference," Mr. Topping explains, "decided how many stories to run, reorganized page one for the second edition, and adjusted the deadlines because of the late hour."

In 1963, Mr. Topping helped write one of the biggest stories of this century. He has described that day this way:

"I was at lunch with the publisher, Arthur Sulzberger, in his dining room on the fourteenth floor when Clifton Daniel, then assistant managing editor, was called to the telephone and returned to say, 'The president has been shot.' We did not have a complete obituary for the young president, John Fitzgerald Kennedy, and when I went to the newsroom on the third floor, I was drafted to write the section devoted to a review of his foreign policy. I was sitting next to Homer Bigart, who was writing the domestic policy review on the front rewrite bank, when Daniel came up to us and said, 'He is dead.' Between 2:00 and 6:30 P.M., Bigart and I wrote a page of *The Times,* grateful for the total preoccupation, and then we walked out to Times Square, where the lights had been dimmed in deference to the dead president."

Certainly page one doesn't carry news of that gravity every day, but Mr. Rosenthal's and Mr. Topping's years of experience as reporters and then editors help them make the judgments necessary to produce a front page that accurately reflects the relative importance of the day's stories.

LAYOUT AND DESIGN

It is five forty-five. The final news meeting has just ended, and news editor Allan Siegal is returning to his desk carrying a list of the seven stories that will run on page one. Working on a special front-page dummy, an 8 1/2" by 11" sheet with column markings scaled to *The Times*'s front page, he does the page-one layout. The editors in the news meeting have indicated the placement of the seven stories according to their relative importance. The most important, called the lead, goes in column six on the far right; the off-lead (the next most important) in column one on the far left. The more important stories are

Allan Siegal completes the page one layout. The photograph on his desk has been discarded in favor of another.

The magnetic mock-up of page one provides Mr. Siegal with a check of the typography (type size and face) and the layout as he has prescribed them on the dummy.

on the right half of the page and "above the fold"—on the top of the page. Tonight Mr. Siegal indicates the size and placement of a map and of a photograph. And he also writes in the sizes and type styles of the headlines. He is paying attention to the visual aspects of the page. "But," he says, "the ultimate decisions are journalistic, not visual."

At six o'clock he is finished. Now copies are made and delivered to all the news desks, the copy desks, the editorial board editors, and to the writers of the news summary and the index, a special boxed guide which appears on the first page of *The Times*'s second section (called the second front).

In his work, Mr. Siegal makes a number of journalistic decisions. One of the most important is setting the news hole—allotting space to each of the news desks on the basis of where the news is happening. He does this after he has received the noon lists from these desks. There is a minimum news hole; it cannot be diminished by advertising space. In fact, when there is more advertising, the news hole increases. But it has not been infrequent for some advertising to be dropped from the paper on a heavy news day.

Basic issues of policy are resolved daily at Mr. Siegal's desk: "Is this in good taste; is the story fair; is the tone right; what were our decisions in similar instances? And on smaller matters of style," he says, "I am the authority. For instance, does this government official use a middle initial; how do we designate the Palestine Liberation Organization?

"I've been interested in language since I was in high school," Mr. Siegal continues. "It took me to the copy

*When there is a
particularly big event,
Louis Silverstein
consults with Mr. Siegal
on the page one layout.*

*Mr. Silverstein discusses
a possible innovation
with his assistant,
Robert Pelletier, as part of
an ongoing review of
the paper's page design.*

desk of *The Times,* but first I was a copy boy. Before I became news editor, I was assistant foreign editor, and I was one of the editors of 'The Pentagon Papers.' Now I'm one of the people who keep the paper afloat; I'm down in the engine room."

Today, because there are two very big stories on page one, Mr. Siegal consults with Louis Silverstein, then an assistant managing editor and corporate art director, who now acts as a special consultant to the New York Times Company. Mr. Silverstein has been involved with art and design from the time he was a child and drew pictures on the sidewalk. He studied at the Pratt Institute in Brooklyn, New York, and at the Institute of Design in Chicago. Mr. Silverstein has been at *The Times* since 1952 and in the last ten to fifteen years has seen major changes resulting in new design. "The paper has moved into the forefront of graphic design," he says. "But," he continues, "the news always comes before design considerations. You want newsworthiness, not just splash."

Members of Mr. Silverstein's staff are assigned to the special sections—for instance: Home; Living; Weekend. They are the designers and art directors of those sections and work with the sections' editors. In addition, an art director lays out the first page of the second section, the Metropolitan Report, and the first few pages of that section. An art director also designs the front page of the Business Day section and works on special graphics in that section. The rest of these two sections are laid out by makeup editors.

"In recent years," Mr. Silverstein continues, "maps and charts have become increasingly important. This material is now called informational graphics. We have nine people working in this area, and their work is increasingly helped by a computer. We feed in data and the computer makes a graph, which the artist then uses as a guide in preparing the finished piece of work for publication."

It is the art director's job to arrange the copy and supporting photographs or other graphic materials in a visually appealing way. "But content and design always must be interrelated," Mr. Silverstein says. "Not everyone who's a good art director is good for newspaper work. You need to know what's going on in the world, you have to be literate, and you must design in context.

"You have to ask yourself," Mr. Silverstein continues, "how can we give the reader a better newspaper? That makes our work meaningful indeed."

EDITING THE REPORT

She arrives at work as the rest of us are having dinner. C. Claiborne Ray, the late slot on the national copy desk, edits copy from 7:45 P.M. until she finishes checking the final edition and leaves at 2:45 A.M. "The only bad thing about this job," she says, "is eating dinner at four in the morning."

She takes over the desk from the dayside head, who has been responsible for supervising the editing for the nine o'clock edition of the national report—the day's national news. It is the first of three main editions—nine, eleven

C. Claiborne Ray begins to edit late national stories when most of the staff has gone for the day.

thirty-five, and one-twenty. With her staff of up to eight, Ms. Ray edits late stories, usually four or five, which come straight to the copy desk (unlike the earlier filings, which get preliminary editing by senior editors at the national desk). "My rim men (so-called, though some are women) get staggered good nights till finally I'm down to my 'middle man,' who leaves at one or one-thirty," she says. "After that, I'm on my own."

In addition to editing raw copy, she and her staff check early edition stories for errors that must be corrected for the eleven thirty-five edition. "In this page-one California story, i.o.u. should be lowercase," she says to one of her assistants. Monitoring wire copy is also part of her job. "If I see a story that obviously should be in the paper, I have a rim editor edit it, and while that's being done, I check to see if we should have a reporter on it and if he can file in time for the edition."

At nine forty-five, page proofs (copies of the paper, the same size as a newspaper sheet) come from the composing room. Evan Jenkins, the night news editor, is spreading his copies out on his desk as Ms. Ray joins him and the makeup editor, Lud Duroska. Together they check to be sure that type hasn't been misplaced, or to make changes for later editions. Such changes go to makeup, and from

With Evan Jenkins (right) and Lud Duroska, Ms. Ray checks page proofs that have been delivered from the composing room.

there to the composing room so the printers will know what changes are coming.

At 10:05 P.M. the copy girl brings the first edition, which has just come off the presses. Ms. Ray looks through it to see that a "short," a brief story that is placed at the bottom of a column, has not been printed twice, or that the same story has not appeared in more than one place. Putting the paper aside, she continues her editing. "Good catch," she says to the rim editor sitting opposite, who has just spotted a serious error. Not sure how much space will be allotted to a story she is scanning (another story may need more space or a photograph may be added), she passes it to an assistant with the instruction, "Add a graf that's bitable." She means, "Add a final paragraph that can be omitted if necessary."

"We edit on the terminals," Ms. Ray explains. "Sometimes we trim with a hatchet, sometimes with a razor blade, but we preserve the reporter's style. And we don't change a lead without consulting the reporter. But we do try to get rid of 'wire-ese.' That's our word for the way some wire copy is written—the result of trying to cram too much or too little into a hard news lead. It's not necessary to get all of the five Ws—who, what, when, where, why —into the first paragraph. What you want is a statement that's a grabber. Years ago a copy editor here told me that we should edit for the man reading his paper standing up in the subway; short paragraphs and simple grammatical structure that sounds like normal English. There are a lot of reporters who write clean copy. They really don't need much editing. But we tell them that the copy editor is probably the only person in the whole world who'll read every word they write.

"What we're aiming for in our editing is fairness, clarity, accuracy, and nonlibelous statements (we check with our legal department; that's what we mean when we say copy has been 'lawyered'). We use a number of reference books: *Webster's New World Dictionary*—it's good on modern usage and proper names; *The Columbia Gazetteer* for place names; *The Times* style book; the Columbia one-volume encyclopedia; the foreign desk uses the Central Intelligence Agency reference in our maps department (the correspondent who's in the middle of a war can't be accurate about geography, so we do that for him); the *Merriam Webster Unabridged Dictionary,* second edition; and our morgue, which is a great research tool. We often send the copy girl for clippings from the morgue. It's called the morgue because it's the place where newspaper clippings, "dead papers," are filed. All of the new material is also put in the computer, but you can't put the whole existing morgue in the computer. Just the references on the president alone might fill a 9′ by 12′ room."

Ms. Ray's first reference book was the *Merriam-Webster Collegiate Dictionary,* which her parents gave her when she was in fourth grade. "We used it at the family dinner table to settle arguments on word meanings." Later she was editor of her high school paper, and after following a liberal arts program in college, worked on small financial papers, "not out of any special interest in finance," she says, "but because that was where I could get a newspaper job." She came to *The Times* in 1977, and after three years on the business and finance desk, moved to the national desk. "I've used all of my liberal arts courses here. It's a great help to have a background of general knowledge. I majored in history, and I think that encourages an objective eye and a critical approach to reports of events. I'm as fascinated by the narrative of the news as I was by the narrative of history.

"When you apply for a copy editor's job, you try out for a week. I found that the most difficult part of the job was writing headlines. It still is. You must be thinking about the head while you're editing the copy. The form we use most often is the architectural, in which each of the two or three lines must be the same length. That's hard. You have to look for synonyms. You need a big vocabulary. Everybody understands how hard it is to get a good head, so the people on the desk help each other. Sometimes I get a head right away, but sometimes it takes fifteen minutes. People who do crossword puzzles are good at this."

It is ten-thirty. They are on a tight deadline now. Ms. Ray passes a late story to a rim man. "Railroad this [rush it] and put a head on it," she says.

At 11:10 P.M., Ms. Ray and one rim man, Peter Lewis, are the only editors still remaining on the copy desk.

THE BUSINESS SIDE

Do the coins we pay at the newsstand for *The Times* pay for its creation and production? Not nearly. "Only twenty percent of our revenues comes from circulation," says John D. Pomfret, executive vice president and general manager. "The other eighty percent comes from advertising. And on newspapers throughout the country, advertising invariably provides the greater revenue, although in some cases circulation contributes a larger part than at *The Times*."

Advertising and circulation are two of the six departments, staffed by over 3,600 people, for which Mr. Pomfret is responsible in his position as manager of the business side of *The Times.* He lists the departments this way:

ADVERTISING
CIRCULATION
OPERATIONS
FINANCIAL
INFORMATION SYSTEMS
EMPLOYEE RELATIONS

Graduating from Princeton University with a degree in history, Mr. Pomfret had no thought of someday managing the business side of a newspaper. In fact, he planned a career in college teaching, but in order to earn some money before entering graduate school, he took a job as a reporter on *The Milwaukee Journal.* Newspaper work appealed to him so much that he abandoned his plan to become a teacher, and after serving two years in the Army in the Korean War, returned to *The Journal* and stayed for ten years. In 1962 he joined the Washington bureau of *The Times* as a labor reporter, later becoming White House correspondent. Four years later he moved to the New York office to work as assistant director of industrial relations, and through a series of promotions over the years, assumed his present position in 1979.

As general manager he is responsible for the work of the six departments he oversees, but he devotes a great part of his attention to maintaining or improving the levels of circulation and advertising. "Big city papers compete with suburban papers for circulation," Mr. Pomfret says, "and there is competition from TV and direct mail for advertising." That is where Mr. Pomfret depends on the efforts of the circulation and advertising departments as well as that complex group called operations, which is principally concerned with production and distribution of the paper. Mr.

John D. Pomfret talks with William O'Fallon, personnel director, who also administers a tuition refund program for Times *employees who are pursuing undergraduate or graduate degrees.*

Pomfret confers frequently with the directors of these three departments, Lance R. Primis, Russell T. Lewis, and J. A. Riggs, Jr., as well as with the directors of financial, information systems, and employee relations.

Mr. Primis, now senior vice president of the *The Times* and head of its advertising department, began his career at *The Times* as a classified ad sales representative. But he too had embarked on quite a different course before that. Graduating from the University of Wisconsin, he was drafted to pitch for the San Francisco Giants but turned down a contract with them in favor of starting a career in business as a field representative for a large paper towel company. A year later he joined *The Times* and soon moved from classified sales to a series of managerial posts in the advertising department. In 1980 he became director of advertising and over the next several years established records in advertising space.

"My father regretted my turning down the Giants' offer," Mr. Primis says, "but I have no regrets. I'm still out there pitching!"

The advertising department is staffed by over 550 people. About half of these work as sales representatives in one of five sections: classified, national, international, financial, and retail. Supporting these sales people is an operations division, which is responsible for getting the ads into the paper, and a marketing division with many responsibilities ranging from research to the creation of promotion and advertising that attract new companies to advertise their products and services in *The Times*.

All these sales efforts require a strong circulation department whose attention is directed toward building a bigger and better readership and getting the paper to it on time. That's the responsibility of Russell T. Lewis, vice president of circulation, and his staff of over 150. They work to maintain and develop *The Times's* audience. Circulation is over 1,000,000 weekdays and 1,600,000 on Sunday. Roughly one-third of these papers are delivered to the five boroughs of New York City, one-third to its suburbs and one-third to the rest of the country, including a special National Edition. It contains all the national, international, and business news that appears in the editions printed in New York, along with the full editorial and Op-Ed pages, and selected cultural, sports, regional, metropolitan, and lifestyle coverage. Mr. Lewis's department is in charge of promoting, marketing, and distributing this edition, which is circulated in the United States outside of the Boston-Washington corridor and is printed in nine cities from coast to coast, using satellite transmission.

The remaining distribution not handled by the circulation department is taken care of by operations, an enormous department that consists of 11 divisions staffed by more than 250 management personnel and over 2,300 crafts people. Under the direction of J. A. "Andy" Riggs, Jr., senior vice president, the operations department works around the clock every day of the year covering everything from the running of the employee restaurant to the running of the presses.

Among the eleven operations divisions are: Purchasing, which buys everything that is used at *The Times*—from newsprint by the ton to paperclips and pastries; Facilities, which takes care of all building and rebuilding; and the Carlstadt, New Jersey, plant, which prints forty percent of *The Times* daily run. Carlstadt, opened in 1976, and the Forty-third Street plant supply papers to New York City, its suburbs, and cities in the Boston-Washington corridor. Carlstadt is one of a growing number of satellite plants big city papers are turning to since they offer more space for trucks and newspaper bundling devices.

The remaining three departments under Mr. Pomfret's supervision, financial, information systems, and employee relations, are smaller but no less crucial to the smooth functioning of the paper. General accounting, budget planning, advertising accounting, credit and customer service departments, and the cashier's office are the concerns of the approximately 200 employees in the financial department, which is overseen by John M. O'Brien, vice president, controller. Their work—as well as the work of every department at *The Times*—depends upon the support of more than 150 people in the information systems department. Headed by Elise J. Ross, a vice president of *The Times* and the highest ranking woman on the business staff, information systems is responsible for computer security and maintenance and for software development and computer operations. There is no area at *The Times* that is not computerized or using computer functions of one sort or another. Employee relations consists of a staff of about 50, who report to a vice president, Howard Bishow. Their primary responsibilities are personnel recruiting, except in the news and editorial departments, and the negotiation and administration of labor contracts, including employee benefits. In addition, they oversee the safety, training, and medical departments, the latter operating twenty-four hours a day to treat *Times* employees for illness or accident.

All these business side procedures are probably not the images we call up when we think of the romance of big city newspapering. And yet they are essential; all of the news functions we have been looking at depend on them.

And finally, the presses couldn't roll without them.

THE PRESSES ROLL

Just as Joseph Herrington, metro slotman, "set" David Dunlap's story, so, throughout the afternoon and evening, slotmen in all the news departments are tapping the set key on their computers, sending edited copy to the Metro-set darkroom in the composing room. Here, one flight above the newsroom and five flights above the press room, there is brisk, purposeful activity as strips of type, really white film with black letters on it, come out of the Metro-set darkroom and are picked up by the makeup printers.

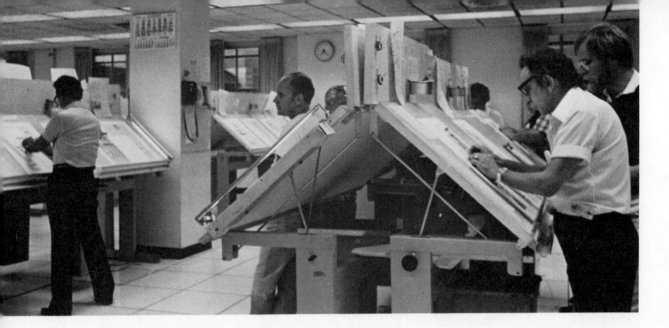

In the composing room, printers place strips of type on the page boards. The clock reads 7:24 P.M. —about an hour and a half to go until the first edition deadline.

It is their job to trim and fit these strips into the appropriate spaces in the page boards on the paste-up tables. At the same time, processed photographs, delivered from the photoengraving department adjacent to the composing room, are trimmed and placed. Makeup editors, scratch sheets (dummies) in hand, come up from the newsroom to make sure that material is being placed on boards as indicated in the dummies. Robert Mallonn, composing room night foreman, is supervising his staff, keeping the process moving to meet quotas, a page closing every minute, that completes everything by 9:00 P.M. Under the clock at the front of the room, the scoreboard shows the closing time of each page.

The copy and photographs for the Dunlap story are being pasted up; the head space, reserved for the headline, is still blank. At 8:15 P.M. the head is delivered, and Mr. Sheridan, who has come up from the newsroom, checks to see that the completed page matches his dummy. Satisfied, he initials it, and so does the printer.

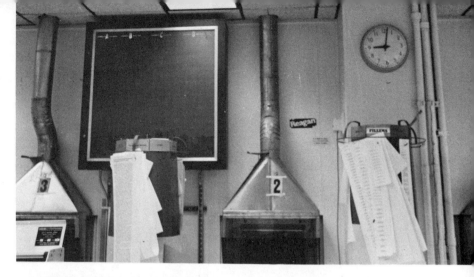

In the composing room as the first edition closes, all page numbers under section letters on the board at the left are out, indicating that all pages have gone to the plate room (page B2 was completed forty-five minutes earlier).

The printer finishes pasting up page B2. The advertisement under his right hand has been placed earlier.

After making certain that the layout matches his dummy, Mr. Sheridan will initial the page.

The technician slips the page board into the scanner, which will electronically transmit an image of the page to the plate room in the basement.

A press man attaches the plate of page B2 to the rotary press.

Now, at eight-thirty, the page is brought to where a laser "scanner" electronically transmits an image of the page to the basement, where plates, the printing surfaces of the page, are made. By 9:55 P.M. the plate of the "starter" page has been attached to the rotary presses, whose revolving cylinders will print the paper. The "starter" (usually page one) is the last to close in the composing room, the last to arrive in the plate room, and

James O'Connell, press room foreman, inspects a printed page on the press.

In a complex traffic pattern, the printed papers are carried by conveyor belt from the press room to the mailroom for bundling.

the last to be fixed to the presses. James O'Connell, press room foreman, gives the start signal, and his crew, wearing the paper hats they have folded from sheets of newsprint to protect their heads from ink droplets, go to work.

The presses roll. You could say they roar; there is a mighty sound, and the air seems to tremble with the tumbling momentum of these giant machines that print 30,000 copies per hour of a 96-page paper. The thundering slows and halts. Mr. O'Connell gives the signal again, and within a few minutes, wave upon wave of *The New York Times* flows along the conveyor and up to the mailroom. There the papers are stacked into bundles, loaded onto the trucks, and at 10:11 the trucks, each holding 10,000 papers, pull out with the first of four editions.

123

The bundled papers are moved by conveyor from the mailroom to the delivery trucks.

In some areas, papers are delivered to doorsteps in predawn darkness.

From now until early morning the paper will be revised, as events dictate, through the eleven thirty-five, one-twenty, and two forty-five editions. Well over a million copies of *The Times,* each containing 250,000 words and consuming 460 tons of newsprint, will have been printed by the time you pick up your copy at the newsstand, doorstep, or open it at the breakfast table.

As the two forty-five edition closes in the composing room, the ranking editor gives "good night" to all those still working in the newsroom. That issue is history.

GLOSSARY

ASSIGNMENT EDITOR.   The editor who assigns stories to reporters.

ASSOCIATED PRESS.   A nonprofit organization that supplies dispatches to newspapers and other news media. *See* **wire copy.**

BEAT.   A particular area covered by a reporter. For instance, police beat, health and hospitals beat.

BOLDFACE.   Dark type.

BYLINE.   The name of the reporter, placed at the top or bottom of the article.

COMPOSING ROOM.   Where the pages of the newspaper are made up—composed—by pasting up all news and advertising material in the designated spaces on the page forms.

COPY EDITOR.   Editor on any of the copy desks who corrects, sharpens, and tightens copy before it becomes type. Copy editors also write headlines.

DATELINE.   The place and date of an article's origin. It appears at the beginning of the first parapgraph.

DAYBOOK.   A list of the next day's activities. It is used by the assignment editor.

DAYSIDE.   The staff that works from morning through to early evening. At *The Times* it is mainly concerned with supervising staff and news gathering.

DUMMY.   Sheet of paper with column markings scaled to page size, showing which space will be used for news and which for advertisements. Also called **scratch sheet.** When completed by a makeup editor, the page shows slugs and headline designations. *See* **slug.**

EDITORIAL.   An expression of opinion, as opposed to the news article, which presents facts without opinion. Editorials appear on the editorial page, separate from news stories.

FEATURE.	A current article, but not hard news, not necessarily written with the most important fact first.
FIRST EDITION.	The first edition off press. At *The Times*, the first edition usually closes in the composing room at 9:00 P.M.
FLAG.	The newspaper's nameplate, or title, on page one.
GENERAL ASSIGNMENT REPORTER	A reporter who is available for general work, as opposed to a beat reporter.
GRAF.	Paragraph.
GRAPHIC.	Chart or diagram to illustrate an article.
HARD NEWS.	Reports presenting the facts of an event objectively and in descending order of importance.
HYPHENATE AND JUSTIFY, OR H AND J.	A process performed by the computer in which the copy is formed into columns, with the right-hand margin made straight by hyphenation and adjusting of the spaces between words.
JUMP.	The continuation of a story from an earlier page.
LEAD (pronounced and somtimes spelled *Lede*).	The beginning of a news story, often but not always containing the five Ws—who, what, where, when, and why.
LEAD STORY.	The most important article on page one. It is placed in the far right-hand column. If it is of great significance, it may have a headline that extends across the entire top of the page.
LOBSTER SHIFT OR TRICK.	The shift that covers late night and early morning.
MAKEUP DESK.	Where pages are dummied by the makeup editors.
METRO EDITOR.	Editor in charge of news in city and suburbs.
MORGUE.	The place where newspaper articles are clipped and filed for reference.
MUG SHOT.	A photograph of the subject's head and neck.
NEWS DESK.	A central authority in the newsroom from which the desks, such as metro, national, and foreign, receive their news holes. The news desk also lays out page one and has overall control of editing and makeup.

NEWS HOLE.	The space reserved for material other than advertising.
NEWS PEG.	An immediate event providing an occasion for printing a feature or situationer.
NIGHTSIDE.	At *The Times,* staff that works during the hours the paper is produced.
OFF-LEAD.	The second most important story on page one. It is placed at the upper left.
OP-ED.	The opinion and column page opposite the editorial page.
PASTE UP.	To place columns of type in the page formats in the composing room.
POSTSCRIPT.	To revise a page between regular edition times.
RAILROAD.	To rush copy into type without detailed editing; an emergency measure.
RAW COPY.	Unedited articles.
RECORDING ROOM.	Where stories dictated by reporters or distant correspondents are recorded on cassette tapes and transcribed.
REWRITE.	The process of writing copy from material phoned in by reporters on the scene where the news is happening.
RIM MEN (OR WOMEN).	Copy editors other than the slotperson. The name derives from copy desks of old, which were horseshoe-shaped.
ROTARY PRESS.	A high-speed press in which a curved printing plate is fitted on a revolving cylinder and the paper is fed between this revolving cylinder and another.
SCANNER.	A machine that passes a laser beam over the page form and moves this image electronically to the plate room.
SCRATCH SHEET.	Diagram for a page of the paper, showing where any ads will go and what news desk will use the page.
SECOND FRONT.	The first page of the second section.
SETTING THE NEWS HOLE	Determining how much space will be reserved for news, as opposed to advertising.

SHIRTTAIL.	A short, related news item added under another dateline at the bottom of an article.
SHORT TAKES.	Brief sections of a story.
SIDEBAR.	A feature appearing in conjunction with a news article, giving human interest or historical aspects of the story.
SITUATIONER.	An article bringing a story up to date in considerable detail.
SKYLINE.	A headline above the newspaper's flag, usually referring to material inside.
SLUG.	The brief heading, usually one word, designating an article or assignment.
SPOT NEWS.	Current news, reported immediately.
STARTER PAGE.	The last page to close in the composing room. When its plate is locked onto the press, the press run can start. Often it is the weather page.
STRINGER.	A reporter who works occasionally for the paper, as opposed to a salaried staff member. Their work was once paid for by length, with knots in a measuring string indicating payment amount.
SUB STORY.	Copy that is substituted for another earlier piece.
TURNAROUND MEETING.	A meeting in the afternoon that turns the work of the daytime editors over to the nightside.
TYPE SIZE.	Size of headline or body type, designated by point. The *Times*'s body type is 8 1/2 point. There are 72 points in an inch.
UPI.	United Press International. A commercial news-gathering organization that supplies dispatches to newspapers. *See* **wire copy.**
WIRE COPY.	Stories supplied to newspapers by news services such as The Associated Press, United Press International, Reuters, and services of other newspapers.
WIRE-ESE.	The jargon that appears in some wire copy, a result of trying to condense too much.